OFF THE RECORD

OFF THE RECORD

WHAT WALL STREET DOESN'T WANT YOU TO KNOW

CRAIG GORDON

WITH STEPHEN KINDEL

CROWN
BUSINESS
NEW YORK

Copyright © 2001 by Craig Gordon

Published by Crown Business, New York, New York.
Member of the Crown Publishing Group.

Random House, Inc. New York, Toronto, London, Sydney, Auckland
www.randomhouse.com

CROWN BUSINESS and colophon are trademarks of Random House, Inc.

Printed in the United States of America

Design by Publications Development Company of Texas

Library of Congress Cataloging-in-Publication Data

Gordon, Craig (Craig C.)
    Off the record : what Wall Street doesn't want you to know / by
Craig Gordon with Stephen Kindel.—1st ed.
        p.   cm.
    1. Investments—United States.   2. Stocks—United States.   3. Mutual
funds—United States.   I. Kindel, Stephen.   II. Title.
    HG4910 .G666 2001
    332.6'32—dc21   2001017342

ISBN 0–609-60779–0

10 9 8 7 6 5 4 3 2 1
First Edition

To all those professional and individual investors who spend the extra time talking to customers, competitors and suppliers before investing. . . .

CONTENTS

CONTENTS

INTRODUCTION

The world of individual investing is one with many different points of view. And one theme that is constantly debated is whether or not an individual investor can buy or sell stocks as well as professional money managers. I believe you can and as proof consider the following three examples:

1. Your next door neighbor, a travel agent, is telling you that the number of cruises she is booking is down dramatically, and cruise lines are giving much bigger discounts to attract travelers this month.
2. Your best friend, an administrator for a cardiology center, is raving about a new product for heart patients called a *stent* that increases the chance of survival in heart patients and lessens the chance of risky surgery.
3. Your college daughter and her friends, who are all members of the Sierra club, have switched their electricity bills to Green Mountain—a company that provides electricity from renewable sources at the same price as the regular utility.

Each is a personal observation that, in addition to looking at the fundamentals of the company involved, provides an opportunity for an individual to have a heads up on a professional money manager. If you know where to look, you will be able to turn up many investment ideas just like these. I will try to teach you how to get them before they are common knowledge.

Wall Street brokerage houses used to be in the business of finding good, new ideas for their clients and conducting research that provides a complete, unbiased picture. Not anymore. Too many firms now have conflicts of interest. In addition to wanting to provide unbiased ideas to their clients, they want to do investment banking for the company involved or to serve institutional clients before individual clients. Many don't want to anger the company. They limit their evaluations to reading company announcements, meeting management, and making conference calls with institutional investors. Only a few actually go out and talk to customers, competitors, and suppliers to confirm or refute what the company executives are saying. Even fewer do it correctly.

For the past 15 years, I have been involved in the institutional finance market doing just that. I am constantly amazed that smart people—practical in many other ways such as seeking a second medical opinion, having a used car checked by a certified mechanic, or asking the opinion of friends before booking a vacation at an expensive resort—do not do this type of kick-the-tires work when buying or selling stocks.

I believe getting a second unbiased check on stocks before buying or selling them gives you a better chance of making the right decision. I believe using our unbiased marketplace approach increases the chance of being right by 5 percent to 10 percent on the buy side and 15 percent to 20 percent when selling a stock.

At OTA/Off The Record Research, we conduct this kind of kick-the-tires research for our clients daily. And our goal is to do it better than anyone else worldwide by spending millions of dollars a year doing this painstaking work. For that effort, our researchers often turn up trends and shifts in market share on companies before much of Wall Street figures out what is going on. And I believe, with a little practice, you can too.

The instances I have outlined are perfect examples of how an individual investor, by keeping his or her eyes and ears open, can see a real story before others and can gain an advantage in making investments. In each of these instances, an individual investor can combine this observation with some fundamental information to see if he or she has a heads up on the market. And by reading this book, I hope you gain the skills to do this a number of times every year you invest. One note of caution for readers of this book: Since we wrote this book, the market has been very volatile and specific examples of valuations may already have changed substantially.

The premise of this book is simple: to give you—the individual investor—the skills to differentiate between what are irrelevant and what are important, unique, observations to help you buy or sell stocks. Whether you are reading this to make your own investment decisions, to learn the market research skill to use professionally or in an investment class, the following pages will help you to structure questions that confirm or dispute your investment thesis, to find useful sources to talk to, and to quickly interpret the information you gather.

In this era of shoot-first, ask-questions-later approach to investing, this book will not show you how to make money in the stock market easily. As a matter of fact, the principles outlined in this book take a lot of effort; however, by using the unbiased marketplace approach and interviewing knowledgeable sources close to you, you can gain a competitive advantage. This book is dedicated to those of you who will make the extra effort to go out and check with unbiased sources to make sure what you have heard from your stockbroker, from a friend, or on the Internet is actually happening.

Welcome to the world of *Off The Record Research*.

OFF THE
RECORD

1

PRECISION INVESTING

How I Find the Profitable Nuggets in the Marketplace

If you invest money in the stock markets, either through mutual funds, or directly, through a broker, you probably do the same things that other investors do. You pick up the newspaper every day, open it to the financial pages, and look up your stocks or mutual funds. Or maybe you subscribe to an Internet stock-tracking or trading service, and your portfolio comes to you on-line every fifteen minutes or so. Maybe you smile because your stocks or mutual funds are going up. Maybe you frown because they fell from the last time you looked at them. But mostly you sigh, because the market isn't giving you any clear indication as to whether you made the right choices.

Certainly, over time, if you stick with the stocks and mutual funds in which you've invested, you'll do pretty well. According to Ibbotson Associates, a Chicago-based research firm, stocks have proven to provide the best return on your money over the long haul, with the least risk. That sounds surprising because everybody knows that the stock market has had periods when it has crashed, but it's true. Stocks are a profitable, low-risk way to make your money grow over the long term.

The problem is always *relative* return. Are you doing better than the market averages? Better than the rate of inflation? Better than your friends? Could you be doing even better? Do you get tired of listening to other people tell you about the great stocks they bought that have gone to record levels, while your mutual funds and stocks are just barely keeping pace with the market averages? Do you get irritated when you hear stories about people making great fortunes in the market, while your stocks seem to ho-hum along? Do you begin to wonder why some people just seem to have better access to information, and why they make better investment decisions?

I'm normally pretty cheerful; but when I think about what a hard time the average investor has keeping up with the experts, I sigh just the way that you do. In fact, if I could put one of those tiny electronic chips that you find on greeting cards—the ones that sing "Happy Birthday," or some such message, into this book—I'd program my chip to heave one great big sigh every time you opened the cover. That's because I feel so sorry for the average investor.

Here's why. I run a company called OTA Off The Record Research (or just OTR) which is based in San Francisco. We supply information to large institutions that invest pension money, mutual-fund money, and private money. The information we supply is designed to help those institutions make better investment decisions, both in buying and selling stocks. OTR Research has been supplying this information for several years and, frankly, we're really pretty good at what we do. Institutions rate us among the best sources from which they regularly buy information, so I guess that means we must be doing something right.

OTR performs marketplace checks. Simply put, we have about 150 people who go out into the marketplace and find out what is going on, who is buying what, how much they are buying, and how often they buy. We look into how a company is doing relative to its competitors, and how an industry as a whole is doing. We translate that information into reports our clients then use to help them determine whether to buy or sell stocks, and which ones. It's that simple. When we do our job well, the institutions make big money and outperform the standard stock indices by which everyone measures performance. When you see a mutual fund or a pension fund that is beating the Standard & Poor's 500 index, chances are that information supplied by us helped them make a buy or sell decision which improved their performance. Even when we don't supply the information, it's probably fair to say that the fund is using a marketplace-check information model similar to ours.

I heave a sigh every time I pick up a newspaper or a business magazine because ordinary investors could be doing much the same thing that I do, and getting better returns. You'd be surprised at how little extra information I'm talking about. One good nugget per year for each of the stocks you own can propel your returns into the upper ranks of performance. Let me give you a few examples.

In the late summer of 2000, everyone was hot on Nokia, the Finnish maker of wireless telephones. It seemed as if everyone had a mobile phone, and that the growth of the industry was going to be endless—both for new subscribers, and for people upgrading their existing phones with new technology and services. People were looking at the mobile-phone market as one large market, but one of our sources pointed out that it was really several markets. There was a business-user market, where demand was stable and even rising, and a student and personal market, which was price sensitive and unstable. Our source told us that Nokia was moving aggressively into the lower end of the market and would therefore have to change its product mix and accept lower profit margins on its products. We advised our clients in July 2000 that Nokia's earnings growth was going to

3

slow, which it did almost immediately. The stock dropped $20 per share, or 33 percent. Our clients, who had sold Nokia before it fell, were protected.

Or take our report on the cruise-line industry. For years, cruise lines have been a major growth industry, with bookings rising at double-digit rates almost every year for a decade. The two pure plays in the business, Royal Caribbean and Carnival, responded the way companies are supposed to when demand is rising: They added lots of capacity. Not only more ships, but much bigger ships, until, by late 1999, capacity began to outstrip demand, which meant that people who were booking cruises could wait longer to book them, thereby driving down the price per cabin. Both cruise lines got hit with a double whammy—they had too many unsold berths, plus they were discounting the cabins they were selling. We began advising our clients about the overcapacity crisis, even as the cruise lines were maintaining that they were selling out their ships. Our findings were in such conflict with Wall Street that some of our best clients questioned our report, until we told them to call their own travel agents and see if they could get a reservation. They could, and very soon thereafter, the entire industry suffered a steep drop in valuation.

Not all of our reports are negative. Sometimes we spot a positive trend in a negative industry. For example, in 1999, there was a lot of talk about the dangers of genetically modified (GM) food. As a result, all of the companies that made GM seeds, such as Monsanto, saw their stock prices hurt by the controversy. But then we discovered Delta and Pine Land, a company that sold GM cotton seeds. People didn't mind wearing goods made of GM cotton. They just didn't want to eat GM foods. So, while the industry as a whole was falling, the firms that bought Delta and Pine Land on our advice saw their shares appreciate 40 percent.

Sometimes we see companies do things that don't immediately make sense. For example, the beer industry has been under competitive price pressures for several years, as the large beer makers—Anheuser-Busch and Philip Morris (Miller) slug it out for incremental market share. As a result, the stocks of both companies remained low because they could not improve their margins. But then during 1999, we noticed that Anheuser-Busch—which makes Budweiser and Michelob—would periodically raise prices in a single region of the United States. If a competitor did not raise them as well, A-B would cut their prices. But if the competitor did not challenge them, the higher prices would stick. We went positive on Anheuser-Busch because we felt that both sides of the beer war wanted and needed profits more than they needed market share. We were right, and A-B's stock rose 50 percent.

These are just a few examples of what happens when you search out critical nuggets of information in the marketplace. You either profit by being in on a share price rise at the beginning, or you avoid a share price fall by getting out before the bad news becomes generally known. Finding such good information takes a little time and effort, but it isn't impossible. We live in an information-saturated society. If you know where to look, you can get all sorts of helpful indicators, even of very large swings in the market.

But instead of hunting for real information, increasingly, investors spend a lot of their time hunting around for tips, which are not the same thing as information. And, increasingly, those tips come from the Internet.

Right now, according to the National Association of Securities Dealers, something like 15 percent of the total volume of shares traded comes from retail investors in electronic trading, who move in and out of stocks in seconds. These short-term investors are like schools of frightened fish, shifting their positions

5

in response to every little upward and downward movement of the stocks in which they choose to invest. Often, those movements are influenced by nothing more than rumors, which are found on the Internet, in investing chat rooms and at financial Web sites that purport to give out real information.

Most of that information is bogus at both ends. It is often wrong about the stocks that are hyped and the stocks that are savaged. There are many stories about small, and micro cap and Internet-based stocks that gyrate wildly based on rumor. In the summer of 1999, a rumor that Source Media (a company that provides streaming content) was the subject of a bidding war between America Online (which went on to merge with Time Warner), and Microsoft. The Source Media's share price soared 50 percent on ten times the normal trading volume. Then the rumors whipsawed the other way, and the stock was traded down. Six months later it was trading at about where it was before the rumors and hype began. Eventually, investors came to look at the company based on a rational business model and priced the stock accordingly, not on the bias of the spin from the rumor mill.

But don't think that this can only happen to the small and thinly traded companies. In early January 2001, Bank of America Corporation, one of the largest banks in the world, was trading along very nicely, fueled by positive actions of the Federal Reserve. Then the California electricity crisis hit, with both sky-high consumer utility bills and rolling blackouts. A rumor spread through the institutional investment community that since the bank, which is very strongly tied to the California economy, held vast quantities of bonds and commercial paper from state based utilities, its portfolio was under stress and that defaults were likely. The bank's stock price, which had closed on January 4 at $51.50, opened the next day at $47.75. That translated to a loss of market capitalization of around $6 billion. Suddenly $6 billion had disappeared. That day the volume of shares traded was almost three times normal. The rumor was taken so seriously that management issued a short statement that began: "We know of no basis to support speculative rumors about our operations. We are conducting business as usual." Well, not quite business as usual if you are issuing statements like that.

Eventually, investors took a long, hard look at the situation and during the next five days of trading the stock recovered to its former position. As the month ended the stock had risen to 54.

The point is not whether Bank of America was a good investment or not. The point is that even a company of its size and reputation can be affected by rumors. Rumors based on neither fact nor rational projection.

Even when people don't fall prey to Internet chatroom hype, they still get their information from the wrong places. One of the most common "sources" of information today is the endless round of talking heads on CNBC and CNN/FN. Every time a stock goes up or down, there is a commentator explaining what is happening, or an analyst or even a CEO or CFO coming forth with an explanation. Well, those aren't explanations, they're *excuses*. By the time these geniuses turn up in the mainstream media with their opinions, the damage has been done. The stock you own has already tumbled, and someone is offering up a reason that seems to make sense. But if it was so obvious after the fact, why wasn't it obvious *before* the fact, when, if you had heard it, you could have taken some action to save your portfolio.

Let me give you a good example of what I mean. In late September 2000, Intel warned analysts that it might have a profits shortfall of as much as $500 million, and the stock immediately lost a big chunk of its value, and set off a whole wave of technology stock selling. Should Intel's news have been a surprise to anyone? Not if you visited Intel's own Web site now and then, it wasn't. Technologically savvy investors who had been to the site as late as mid-August knew that Intel was already having problems with its latest Pentium chip, and had recalled an existing chip because of problems. Those delays and recalls translate directly into lost sales, because computer manufacturers have to seek alternate sources, such as chips from Advanced Micro Devices (AMD). The information was out there for anyone to find. You just had to know where to look. But the mainstream media didn't bother to look, and instead were caught scrambling to come up with excuses to explain Intel's woes.

The rumors and hype, and the inadequacy of the mainstream media are among the reasons I decided to write this book about marketplace checks. You spend too much time and work too hard to accumulate money for investment to just give it up to a marketplace made up of people who care so little about how hard you work for your money.

I'm not saying that the Wall Street community is irresponsible. Overwhelmingly, the people who run brokerages and sell-side firms are honest and responsible. But they aren't terribly interested in you, no matter what their commercials say. They are interested in moving money around, in investment banking, and in earning fees for their companies. You are just a fee machine for Wall Street. If you want to earn real money, you have to take real responsibility for your money.

We live in a high-speed world, an environment where opportunities can seemingly be lost in seconds. I say seemingly, because most of those opportunities are more apparent than real. The reality is a little different. Much of the real movement of stocks is based upon information that filters its way into the marketplace, not by Internet-spawned rumors. But even if Internet day trading didn't exist, you, the average investor, would still need all the help you could get. There are better returns to be had, and with a little knowledge and discipline, you can achieve those returns, whether it's on your mutual funds or on the stocks you purchase directly.

Part of what makes investing in stocks seem to be more scary than it actually is comes from the fact that the stock markets yo-yo every day, in what appears to be a meaningless gyration. In fact, that motion is driven both by information, which we'll talk about in the next chapter, and by the following factors dealing with basic issues of supply and demand:

A. Net new money. Every month, working Americans contribute between $20 billion and $30 billion to their retirement portfolios, in the form of investments in their 401(k) plans, IRAs, Keoghs, SEPs, and a host of other government-supported, tax-advantaged programs. Out of this supply, there is also a steady stream of stock sales, mutual-fund redemptions, and shifting of money from stocks to cash, as people meet their retirement or other personal needs. The net supply of money—inflow minus outflow—goes into stocks, bonds, Treasury bills, real estate, and mutual funds. Right now, inflow exceeds outflow by a considerable margin, so that as more money comes into the markets, it pushes stock prices upward.

B. Security supply. While money is flowing in, the supply of securities in which to invest fluctuates. New securities are issued as Initial Public Offerings of new companies (IPOs), as new stock issues of existing companies, as new corporate and municipal bonds, and as the regular issuance by the U.S. Treasury. At the same time, many companies announce stock buybacks, caught as they are between rising amounts of cash on hand and a lack of rational investment opportunities. According to the Securities and Exchange Commission, despite the steady flow of new issues, mergers by large-capitalization companies have sufficiently outpaced newer issues of small-capitalization—and small stock-issuing—companies, so that for the past decade, the net supply of securities in which the public can invest has actually decreased by about 1 percent annually. That small but constant drop also helps to buoy the stock markets.

C. Earnings. Earnings are the reason you invest. If the company whose stock you buy has a steadily rising stream of earnings, then it is more desirable than a company which is losing money, or whose earnings are flat, or rising slowly. If your company's earnings are superior to those of other companies, the demand for the stock of your company goes up, and consequently the price rises. If the earnings are inferior, or if the company is losing money, then demand for the stock goes down and the price falls. It's that simple.

D. News events. Every bit of news is analyzed by a horde of media analysts for its potential impact on the economy. This includes pseudo-forecasting, such as the effect of National Football Conference or American Football Conference Super Bowl victories on the rise and fall of the stock market, and the rise and fall of dress hemlines and their effect on the market. More serious events, such as the resignation of a Treasury secretary, can have an impact on the broad market. In addition, companies change all the time. They make changes in their management teams, hiring new chiefs and firing old ones. They announce changes in strategy, or they buy companies. Or they allow themselves to be acquired. All of this news is analyzed, and factored into the expectations of every investor.

E. Rumor. Because stock and bond prices reflect the present value of future expectations, for every fact available to the market, there are ten rumors and illogical interpretations, just as there are vastly more "paper barrels" of oil trading in the oil futures market than there is real oil available. As information becomes known, rumors evaporate, to be replaced by newer rumors farther out in the future. If macroeconomic information is the broad wave on which the market rides, rumors are the little eddy currents, the tips of the waves, which splash up against investors on the beach, sometimes tickling their ankles, sometimes knocking them off their feet.

If you look at the sources of information, and the frequency with which they come to the market, you'll find a curious thing to be true: Real, hard information comes to the market no more than a few times a year, with the exception of flow of funds, which is announced monthly. Every other factor which might influence the price of any given stock—all the bits of "news," rumor and innuendo—comes pouring in daily. To put it in an exaggerated form, Wall Street is forced to confront the truth only four times a year. The rest of the time, the stock markets exists on fears, hopes and dreams.

That's where our company comes in. In between the models and hard knowledge of the analysts, and the rumors and "news" that influence stock prices over the short term, there is the process that we call "marketplace checks," the system we use to supply information to the clients who depend on us for superior returns. Marketplace checks are a little like an extra piece of a jigsaw puzzle—we get information from lots of different sources and use it to construct a model of the economy—but it's also like news, because it's local and it happens every minute of every day.

We take in a lot of information, but we don't have to wait until the end of the quarter to use it. OTR has a kind of fluid macroeconomic and company model that changes daily, based on real information, not unsubstantiated rumors and half-truths.

We ask three basic questions. First, "How is the industry doing?" Is it growing or slowing? Are there macroeconomic factors which are moving it? For instance, when looking at the oil industry, the trend toward fuel-efficient automobiles, or toward gas-guzzling SUVs has an effect on consumptions that you had better understand. In good times of growth, we have a saying,

"A rising tide lifts all boats." You must know how your industry is affected overall.

The second question we ask is, "Within the industry, how is a specific company doing?" Is it gaining market share? Is it outperforming its competitors? Does it have a superior product? Are other companies releasing competitive products?

This question separates the ultimate winners from losers. Ideally, one likes to find the company which is outperforming its competitors in an industry which is growing. Most of the time, that does not happen. In fast-growing markets, there are usually a great many competing companies. The best strategy is to invest across the industry, and then to identify those that break out. We see this pattern in every time and age. At the birth of the industry, there were hundreds of computer companies, and no one could tell which would be successful which would be gobbled up, and which would fall away. The railroads, the automobile industry, the oil industry, the airlines, the computer manufacturers, the software makers—all experienced this curve. Ten years later, winners and losers were clear.

The third question we ask is, "Are there any material items of interest?" This question may seem to be broad, but as you study an industry, you get a feel for what might affect it. A good example is the controversy on genetically modified (GM) foods. Looking at the industry, the producers, and the first line of consumers (the farmers who buy GM seeds) one would have thought this was a wonderful investment opportunity. It looked as if even the science was on our side. But modifying food, and the cries of "Frankenfoods," along with the outbreak of mad-cow disease in England, created an ultimate consumer resistance. Even if not true, many of the stories scared people and their governments. Suddenly the genetic-seed business was not the slam-dunk success it once appeared to be. You must be on the alert for things that seemingly are only passingly related to your investment focus. That gives us a real edge in a marketplace that is always looking for new information on which to base decisions.

Marketplace checks do not predict stock prices. Nobody can really do that with any great reliability, although people have been trying to "read" the market for decades, the way a soothsayer purports to "read" a crystal ball. Individual investors like you pay dearly for such readings. All told, you are collectively spending nearly $500 million a year on newsletters, advisory services, charting services, and the like, not to mention the billions more you spend indirectly carrying the analysts of large brokerage houses through the fees you pay, and the additional billion dollars or so you spend on financial newspapers such as *The Wall Street Journal* or such magazines as *Money* or *Worth* or *Smart Money*.

I would never be so presumptuous to say that all of that money you're spending is wasted. It isn't. There is a lot of valuable information in the media, and often, good analysis in specialized financial-information services. But much of it is contradictory and, in the end, too much information is just noise.

In information theory, noise is anything that interferes with the ability of a signal to travel over a line to its destination. Claude Shannon is a mathematician who, back in the 1940s, worked at Bell Labs. There he developed the basic ideas of information theory. Shannon's theories were meant to help the phone company make better use of its equipment, and to point the way for improvements in service. But Shannon's simple theory turned out to have very wide implications because it deals with how information moves through channels. When Shannon first conceived his theory, the information was pulses of electricity that moved over wires. If you pushed too much information over a wire, you created interference, and when you had enough interference, the "noise" level began to rise, until you could no longer hear a phone conversation.

Shannon was a brilliant man who quickly realized that his theory had other uses besides improving phone service. He understood that the transactions between individual investors and their brokers were like telephone conversations, and that the information which influenced those decisions was just like the reasons why people made phone calls. Shannon thought that if you could find a way of canceling out the noise—all of the contradictory bits of information that influenced the prices of stocks—you could make a fortune as an investor. So in the early 1950s, Shannon left Bell Labs and went to work on finding a formula that would make him rich. To his great chagrin, he failed and, after a couple of years, he turned to a simpler, though so far still-unsolved problem: teaching a machine to juggle.

Back in the 1980s, Wall Street began to turn its attention to a different version of Shannon's idea. Really smart people on Wall Street began to figure out that while they could pick out good information—such as a company's earnings report—and that they could discard truly awful information—such as a rumor that Procter & Gamble's trademark is a symbol of Satanism. (Note however that in spite of the sheer absurdity of this rumor, P&G took it seriously enough to issue a denial on its Web site which included the support of Reverends Jerry Falwell and Billy Graham, and the archbishop of Cincinnati.) Still, there was a lot of stuff in the middle that might or might not have an impact on prices. They also began to discern that there were patterns even in the seeming chaos of daily trading, and that sometimes one form of trading pattern prevailed, and a little later, another form of trading pattern would begin to take over.

With those two notions driving the thinking of some of the smartest people on Wall Street, they came to a blinding realization: It didn't matter what the value of the information was, or what the trading pattern was. It was who discovered it first and could adjust his or her trading practices to reflect each new input who would be the most successful. That insight launched an all-out arms race on Wall Street, as firms began to invest billions of dollars in private satellite networks for their traders, in super-computers that could crunch numbers at near–light speeds, and in high-end software programs that could catch each little inflection and direct the traders to make adjustments.

Often, the programs traded without human intervention and, for a while, the best of them made money. But just as Shannon failed to eliminate unwanted noise, all Darwinian algorithms and trading programs that were supposed to make one Wall Street firm or another a dominant power have fallen by the wayside.

Why is that?

I believe that all of these very expensive and very sophisticated systems fail because—ultimately—information *does* matter. Speed is vital once you have the right information. But if your information is second-rate, a bad decision executed rapidly is just money thrown down a rat hole at a faster pace than your competitor can discard it. Since many of the little shifts in the market which trading programs are designed to catch and respond to are based solely on rumors, after a while, the effects of rumor and pseudo-news will cause market distortions. When a real piece of information is introduced into the mix, the shift is so rapid that the trading programs cannot react to it in time, and they fail.

That is why we have developed a business whose sole purpose is to dig out real information. Real information will always triumph over rumors, because at the end of the day, it can be confirmed in a way that rumors and innuendo never can be. Marketplace checks are real information, and whether the information comes in the form that we supply to our clients, or the kind that I will teach you how to develop for yourself, it is information that you can use to gain leverage and advantage in your investing. I won't turn you into a soothsayer, but knowledge *is* power. If I can help you develop a bit of knowledge about a company and its industry that nobody else has, and you use that knowledge to make a better investment decision, you've suddenly done something you probably thought was impossible. You will have put yourself on a level plane with some of the best and the brightest on Wall Street.

I'm not going to kid you. What this book will teach you is not going to be easy for you to absorb. It will require that you rethink the way you invest and the way you take in information. If you want to become a successful investor, you will have to develop a level of discipline about investing that, right now, you probably bring only to your profession. You may be an individual investor, or you may belong to an investment club. Either way, there are lessons in this book that you can use. I'll tell you right now that if you belong to an investment club and you use the methodologies that I am going to teach you, your club's return has the potential to improve substantially because the more people who are involved in ferreting out information and analyzing it together, the more likely it is that you can come to the right conclusions. That's just because a group can gather and analyze more information than one individual person. As my own company has grown from just a handful of people to more than 150, the quality of the information that I have been able to supply to large institutions has improved markedly each year.

But even if you decide to go it alone, I can show you how to use marketplace checks to improve the way you process the information that's already available to you through conventional sources, and how to apply a marketplace-check rationale to every bit of information you take in daily. You'll learn how to improve what you keep and what you discard, so that you will become smarter about the market in every way.

And that is bound to make you a better investor.

2

DON'T DIVERSIFY

*Why You Should Put All of
Your Investment Eggs in a Few Stocks*

Much of the information that comes through conventional information sources, such as CNBC, CNN/FN, *Money* magazine and newspapers, is based upon the behavior of institutional investors. Top money managers are always being quoted; their picks form any of the recommendations that fill the papers and airwaves. As a result, you probably think that institutional investors buy stocks the same way that you do, except that they have better information or are more sophisticated.

If you think that, you are wrong. You certainly know what the money managers are investing in, and you probably also know some of the reasons why they've picked one stock over another. But you don't know their objectives, so you don't know what forces are at work when they sell them unexpectedly, leaving you holding the bag. Since we serve institutional clients, I thought that I'd talk a little bit about how large institutions work. The insights you get from this discussion can help your own investment decisions. It will certainly help to explain why you shouldn't automatically accept some money manager's pick as your own, and why you need to develop different strategies in picking your own stocks.

Let's look at an institutional investor from its beginning. A company forms a pension fund, for example, or an investment company forms a mutual fund, and begins to raise money for it. From the moment the fund is formed, it has expenses: office space, telephones, computers and software, the salaries of analysts, clerical help, the trading desk, lawyers and regulatory watchdogs, people to keep records and dozens of other specialized employees. Then there are travel expenses for the analysts and money managers, so they can visit the companies they cover. All of this money is going to be subtracted from the money that the fund earns. So, right away, a fund has two types of return: gross (the overall return) and net (the return minus overhead). There are funds, like Vanguard, which are legendary for their ability to keep overhead low, so that more of the money goes to the investors. Others depend on their ability to generate superior returns, and worry less about their overhead.

Once the fund is up and running, its analysts and managers begin the process of looking for stocks to buy. They are generally not looking for huge winners, but rather, stocks that will go up at a rate that is slightly better than an index like the Dow Jones Industrial Average, or the Standard & Poor's average of 500 stocks. There is a simple reason for this. In order for fund managers to know whether they are doing well, there must be a benchmark for comparison. The indices are a common and simple shorthand of performance that every investor understands, and it is a terrific selling tool as well. If your fund beats the Dow or the S&P 500, you are doing better than the market as a whole, and your success brings more money into your fund.

Because these funds have hundreds of millions—often billions—of dollars available to buy and sell stocks, they do not pay the same kinds of fees that individual investors pay. Large institutions have enormous clout on Wall Street, and they use it. In addition to paying very low fees, their business is sufficiently valuable that Wall Street firms give the funds all sorts of so-called advantages, such as specialized research and access to analysts, and access to Initial Public Offering shares, and best execution on trades that could lower the price and institution pays by 5 to 25 cents per share. At OTA Off The Record Research we have one trader, Rob Santangele, who is known on the New York stock exchange floors for pushing the specialist far beyond a reasonable effort until he is absolutely certain he has obtained the best possible price for his institutional client. Rob serves as a role model for the rest of our desk. This combination of low fees, extra effort by traders on the desk for institutions, and extra perks helps to lower the cost of owning a stock for an institution.

What do I mean by that? Let's say you buy 200 shares of a stock at $50 a share for $10,000, and you pay $350 to your full commission broker. You will also pay him $350 when you sell the stock. That's a total of $700, or 7 percent of the value of the purchase. In order for you to make any money at all on the stock, it has to go up by more than 7 percent, or higher than $53.50. If the stock rises to $60 per share, your 20 percent gain is reduced to only 13 percent when you sell. That forces you to hold onto shares longer than you might like.

That high transactional cost is what accounts for the rise, first, of discount brokers like Charles Schwab, and now, of Internet brokers like E*TRADE. By lowering your transactional cost down to less than $10, they are hoping that you will trade more frequently, so that they will earn the same amount of money from your account as if they charged you the same high fees as a traditional broker. But remember: No matter how little you are paying for your trades, the institutions are paying even less, so they can move in and out of stocks on gains of a few pennies, and still make money.

As a result, institutions trade in two ways, while you can generally trade in only one way. They own stocks in their portfolios both for the long haul and for short-term day trading. Institutional holders look for stocks that have some volatility to them, and then use their computers and trading desks to move in and out of these stocks on a minute-by-minute basis. A stock may rise or fall only one point by the sound of the trading bell, but it may have gyrated as much as 20 percent or more on an intraday basis. An astute trader can capture a significant portion of that rise and fall, and carry the results over to the overall profitability of the fund. You might attempt to mimic the fund's performance by holding the same stocks, but you are destined to fail. You are holding through the month, while the funds are trading for fractional gains every day.

Aside from transaction costs, what separates you from the institutions is volume and movement. The 100 or 200 shares you might buy or sell on a given day are nothing compared to the hundreds of thousands of shares that the institutions trade every hour. For a very long time, institutions had to either find other large institutional buyers to purchase their blocks of stock, which required a very sophisticated trading-desk operation, or they had to break their blocks up into smaller units and move them into the market gradually, a bit at a time.

The rise of day trading by individuals has changed much institutional activity. Because day traders are constantly moving in and out of stocks, even though their buy and sell orders are small, there are often enough of them that order matching by the institutions is much easier. If a fund is holding 10,000 shares of a heavily traded but thinly capitalized stock—a definition that fits many Internet stocks—it is not very hard for a desk trader at a fund to pour shares into the transactional flow and let the day traders snap them up. So, while many people lament the arrival of day trading and its casinolike mentality, the day traders have actually increased the liquidity of certain

20

stocks, making it easier for the large institutions to make money. As far as I know, nobody has quantified exactly how much day trading has helped the institutions by increasing liquidity, but I would bet that the huge ramp-up in volume over the past two or three years has directly benefited the performance of many funds.

In addition to volume, increased trading also increases volatility, which also benefits the larger funds. In the last chapter, I told you about the great Wall Street arms race of the 1980s. Companies began investing heavily in supercomputers and black-box trading systems that could spot subtle movements in the market and execute buy and sell decisions on an automated basis, making money on even tiny price moves. As volume increases, the opportunity to profit goes way up because there is more movement in the price of stocks.

If you've ever been to the Bay of Fundy, in Canada, you'll understand what I'm talking about. The Bay of Fundy is a tidal bore. While the tide on the surrounding beaches might rise and fall a few feet each day, the tide in the bay rises and falls more than twenty feet because the volume of water coming in at the mouth of the bay is much greater than the space for it at the back of the bay. Similarly, a rising tide of trades pushes more stock through a market that is no larger than it was before the market increased, so the price swings are greater. The people with the fastest trading engines—the institutions—harness most of that energy. When Internet stocks fell on April 14, 2000, the resulting complaint was not about the tumble in prices, but of the falloff in trading that followed it. If you are an institution, it is much harder to make money in the market if there is diminished stock flow.

One of the ways that large funds are prevented from completely dominating the price-setting mechanism is through SEC rules which limit the amount of investment a fund can make in a company. Most funds adhere to a 5 percent rule, which means that they can invest no more than 5 percent of their funds in any one stock. They can own more than 5 percent of the company, but their investment cannot exceed 5 percent of the fund's total capital.

Why do funds adhere to this rule? The most important reason is fiduciary responsibility. As a custodian of other people's money, institutions and mutual funds have to act responsibly, lest they be fined by the SEC. If a manager puts too many eggs—invested funds—into too small a basket, if the company gets into trouble, the fund will wind up taking a bath because it will not be able to sell its shares. So, once again, the fund management is geared toward maintaining sufficient liquidity so that the fund can make trades pretty much continuously. You, on the other hand, don't have such problems. You can put all of your investments into a single stock if you are confident in it, and get a much better return. The diversification that money managers encourage does you little good when the market is surging ahead, and the stock you've invested in is on a tear.

Still another difference between the way professionals invest and the way you invest is in the way you do research. As I noted earlier, large institutions receive their market-making news hours before you do. That gives them an advantage that you are going to be able to neutralize only with marketplace checking. But the research advantage that institutions enjoy is not limited solely to timing. It is also a question of depth. When *Institutional Investor* puts together its all-American research team, analysts are judged on their responsiveness to the needs of their clients. In fact, that is probably the most important single criterion, and not the quality of the research. An analyst who digs out a nugget of information that could lead to an investment decision, who then calls his or her clients at 5:00 A.M., before the markets open, is far more valuable than someone who waits until the morning call to release a piece of news.

Analysts who serve the institutional community also cover their companies in much greater depth. Rather than the generalized buy, sell, and hold recommendations that retail analysts make, institutional analysts will spend a lot of time with the chief financial officers of the companies they cover, attempting to know something about the quality of the earnings the company is going to generate.

What is quality of earnings? It is the *source* of the earnings, rather than the amount. The best earnings come from rising sales and declining expenses. The next-best earnings come from the investments made with retained earnings from previous quarters. After that, earnings may come from the sale of a subsidiary, or the manipulation of inventory, or a host of accounting tricks, some of which are considered to be legitimate, and many others that are considered to be questionable.

Companies can sometimes massage their quarterly earnings upward by persuading their own customers to accept more inventory in this quarter than they are actually paying for. Once the inventory is shipped, it is "booked" as a sale, even though no money has actually changed hands. The company sends its customer a bill, with the clear understanding that the invoice will not be paid until well into the next quarter. If a company does this sort of thing occasionally, it can usually get away with it. But when prebooking sales ("flooding channels") becomes a way of life, there comes a moment in the company's existence when it is going to have to restate its earnings to account for the fact that the numbers were not real. At that point, the chief financial officer or the CEO are usually looking for another job. A good fund manager knows what to look for in these situations, and will have exited the stock long before you do.

While the chief financial officer may give the fund manager positively biased information, you, on the other hand, have an unbiased marketplace-check system to keep you from being burned. Let me give you an example. In a late May 2000 Flash

Report, we told our clients about the poor sales of Callaway Golf's new ball: "Early consumer response to Callaway Golf Co.'s new golf ball, Rule 35, has been mixed, according to eight golf retailers. Most sources had expected initial sell-through to be stronger, and said its high price was the biggest stumbling block. Although ball demand had been expected to outstrip supply, six sources said they had all the supply they needed."

Now, there is nothing here to suggest that Callaway is doing anything that it shouldn't. They've put a product on the shelves, expecting consumers to buy it, and consumers have been turned off by the high price. But, read another way, that six suppliers said they had all the supply they needed, you might infer that Callaway was flooding its retail channels. Under those circumstances, you'd be automatically wary, and would look at the company's quarterly earnings statement to see what they have to say about the overproduction and filling of retail channels.

As a marketplace checker, you have the chance to notice things, and then to correlate them with what might appear on a company's earnings statement or its balance sheet. Are your golfing friends using the new Callaway ball, or the new Nike ball, or are they just buying what they always used? If what you've observed and what buyers are telling you does not add up to what the company is saying, you probably have spotted a legitimate disjuncture in the information flow of the market, and can buy or sell on that news.

Another major difference in the research that is given to institutions is the financial modeling behind the numbers. While you struggle with a handful of financial indicators, large institutions have computer models that look for all sorts of subtle distinctions between and among companies. Analysts or fund managers who read these financial tea leaves look at their roster of investments from a different perspective. It is not particularly difficult for managers to plug in existing investments as well as competing stocks, and then have the results displayed graphically, so that they do not have to crunch any numbers beyond the initial input.

You, on the other hand, are working with a spreadsheet that you've built by hand. *Investor's Business Daily,* which is the closest thing that the average investor has to an equalizer, uses a proprietary model that contains more than 150 different variables, in order to provide its own lists of hot stocks. But in the absence of the model, you have to accept the hypothesis, and even the best models require more art than science by the user.

This seems to leave the average investor at a disadvantage to the institutions, but, there is more art than science in interpreting the numbers that the models give you. It's sort of like playing Free Cell on your computer. Sometimes you get on a roll and win game after game. Then, just as suddenly, you can't win at all. Statisticians have a name for this: It is called "regression to the mean," and it is the one rule that really separates fund managers from average investors. Because the investing game is loaded so heavily in favor of large institutions, it is easier for a fund manager to have a longer run of success than an individual investor. But longer does not mean permanent, except in certain unusual cases, such as Fidelity Magellan's Peter Lynch in the 1970s and 1980s. Remember the statistic we gave you in Chapter 1? Most of the mutual fund managers—more than 80 percent of them, according to Morningstar, the Chicago company that tracks mutual fund performance—do not do as well as the S&P 500. They *underperform* the market. Thus, with all their research and all their technology, they regress even *below* the mean.

Why should that be? I've already told you some of the reasons. Poor performance begets more poor performance. When a fund manager is not doing well, investors withdraw money from the fund, which causes a rise in marketing expenses to attract new money, which in turn causes the fund's overall return to fall until that new money is invested properly.

Second, fund managers, by sticking to structured diversification of their portfolio, limit their own opportunities to earn more money. If a fund is invested heavily in, say, international or high-technology stocks, the volatility in those markets increases the downside risk as much as it increases the upside potential. If you are a fund manager who wants to keep his or her job, would you put more or less money into those high-volatility stocks, even if the fund was dedicated specifically to those sectors? If you answered, "More money," you would be wrong. Nobody on Wall Street gets rewarded for being audacious, and few people are penalized for being cautious. If the fund underperforms, they mail out a notice with the quarterly report that extols the fiduciary responsibility of the manager in a volatile market.

One final difference between institutions and individuals. You pay taxes on your investment successes. Funds and institutions don't. Mutual funds pass on the taxes to their shareholders. When you receive dividends from a mutual fund, which is your share of the fund's profits, you pay the taxes. You also have to pay taxes on your share of the capital gains of the fund at the time the gains are realized, unless the fund is protected by being inside your IRA, 401(k), SEP, or Keogh plan.

That tax bite immediately lowers your personal return and causes you to hold onto stocks and fund shares longer than you might otherwise. Why? Because if you buy and sell quickly, the tax bite is the same as your personal income-tax rate, but if you hold for long-term capital gains, the tax hit is lower. Congress is constantly tinkering with both the rate and the holding period for capital gains. But it has been a fundamental precept of government tax/economic planing to encourage people to hold onto their investments to encourage people to become long-term savers, on the assumption that if people hold onto their stocks, they will do well enough over the long haul, and will at least outpace inflation.

Now that you have some understanding of how large institutions work, ask yourself, "Is there anything in the funds' behavior that I can emulate? Is there anything I can do to pump up my own portfolio's return?" The answer is largely no. In fact, following the behavioral pattern of the typical fund manager can get you into a lot of trouble.

Let's start at the beginning. A fund manager has overhead expense. You don't—or, at least, you don't credit it to your portfolio and you can't deduct your overhead from your taxes, unless you are viewed by the IRS as a professional investor. On one hand, that's an advantage to you, because more of your gross profits become net profits. This should make you feel better. On the other hand, lots of those overhead expenses are real, and since you cannot deduct them, you wind up paying for them.

Also, your costs are higher than an institution's—higher costs in both the price you pay for the stock and the absolute commission you pay. Institutions placing orders for hundreds of thousands of shares in a single trade can get a price of 12 to 25 cents per share better than an individual. You, on the other hand, with a trade of even a few thousand shares, are going to pay more. There is no way you can get around that fact. You can limit the amount that you have to pay by buying and selling on-line, but even with minimal transaction costs you will still lose out on price in the buy and sell. On a $50 stock, if you trade on-line, a rise to $60 per share will net you an 18 percent gain, not a 20 percent gain. That's better than the 14 percent we spoke of earlier, but it's not yet good enough.

Institutional money managers diversify their portfolios into different classes of investments because the profits they produce are used for different purposes. Presumably, you are not investing in order to simply take profits and spend them. That is the equivalent of redemptions in a fund. If you get the gain quickly and sell quickly, then you have to pay tax at your existing marginal rate, which might be as high as 38 percent. So, on top of the $1 you gave up in trading expenses, you are now going to give up as much as another $3.80 to Uncle Sam. That's 48 percent of the total gain, which lowers your overall gain from 20 percent down to 11.4 percent. That's still way ahead of inflation, but it's not nearly as terrific as if you had managed to keep the whole 20 percent.

Fund managers are rated on how well they do against standard indices. You aren't. It's nice to do better than the Dow or the S&P 500, and it gives you some real bragging rights among your friends to be able to say that your portfolio rose 40 percent in value last year. But what you really need to do is to outperform the rate of inflation. It is inflation that erodes the value of your money over time and makes you feel uncomfortable in the middle of the night, as you worry whether you'll have enough money to survive a very long old age. It is inflation that erodes your standard of living and makes you feel a little bit poorer each day. And it is inflation that your portfolio needs to conquer, whether the indices are roaring ahead or lagging behind. Your choices of investments should always be based on beating the rate of inflation by at least double, no matter what the stock markets are doing. If the indices are performing exceptionally well and you can outperform them, so much the better, because it just builds up your wealth cushion so much more. But beating the indices should not be your immediate goal.

In order to beat inflation, you have to turn away from the fund manager's strategy of absolute portfolio diversification, and begin to think about making selective bets based on the unique material time related information that you acquire. Diversification is a wise move. Putting all your eggs in one basket (especially a tiny basket of only one or two stocks) is foolhardy. Remember: You can have all the right information but, because of circumstances beyond your control, things can go wrong. A company which has everything going for it can experience parts shortages because of an earthquake near a supplier halfway around the world. With the international economy, transit strikes in France, and crop failures in West Africa can have devastating effects on a single investment.

Suppose your fabulously famous and universally loved corporate spokesman falls to some scandal. These things happen. Most of the time, they do not. Good planning, superior products, and service usually result in success. And those who identify success early and are willing to invest generally prosper. This is what you can do. Most of your portfolio should be invested in a diversified manner. But you can still have a tremendous upside by working to identify real opportunities within a narrow field, to make some significant investments. You need to concentrate on a narrow area to be able to identify those hidden opportunities.

Here's why. This book will show you how to use information to your advantage. Well, just how many insights, in how many different businesses, do you think you're going to be able to discover? At OTR, we limit our research to about 300 stocks, the ones that are most widely held by portfolio managers. We know that institutional holders have stakes in virtually every stock in the marketplace; but by concentrating our efforts in a narrow range, our results will be better, and our clients will continue to pay us.

It's the same for you. If you take a scattershot approach to research you stand a much greater chance of missing a salient piece of information than if you become an expert in a narrow range of stocks. That's what I meant by precision investing, which I discussed in Chapter 1.

Do not misconstrue what I am telling you here. Most people tell you that if you have to concentrate on one area, then pick high technology, because that's where the gains were greatest. That is not what I am saying. It is difficult to get good information on technology companies, precisely because they are the most dynamic in terms of changing market share. If you know something about computers or the Internet or telecommunications, then by all means begin to follow tech stocks in greater detail, using the marketplace-checking processes I show you.

But you should know that you can make money in practically any sector, if you know the sector well enough. Some of the best-performing funds are stodgy bond funds, because the managers are minutely sensitive to even the slightest fluctuations in interest rates and milk those changes for all they are worth. You can make money in low-P/E industries like the automotive sector, or you can make money in high-P/E sectors, like high technology. It doesn't matter what the sector is. What matters is the amount of expertise you can develop in the sector, and your ability to take advantage of what you know. If you can find one nugget of information per month, and trade on that information, you will outperform the market consistently. And if you find one nugget a year that presages a large movement in the stocks you follow, you will beat the Wall Street professionals.

Concentrating your portfolio works well when you do your homework, when your team and the panels you develop are all working in sync. It will add immeasurably to your life experience simply because you will have developed an entirely new dimension of expertise, and your success may give you the incentive to expand into a new sector. If you are investing in the automobile industry, it is only a short jump to the auto-parts industry. If you are investing in airlines, it is only a short jump to all of the transportation companies that deliver by air, such as FedEx and UPS. As you become more knowledgeable, more opportunities will open up for you. That's probably the greatest advantage of marketplace checks, beyond the money it might make you as an investor.

3

THE FOUR INFORMATION SOURCES YOU CAN'T INVEST WITHOUT

In order to be successful, you have to acquire intimate knowledge of the companies and industries in which you plan to invest. This knowledge traditionally has four components:

A. Knowledge of company management. You can study all the balance sheets you want to but, ultimately, the quality of the decisions made by a company's management are what counts. If they are careful with expenses, it shows up on the Income Statement. If they spend money on research and development, it shows up as a steady stream of new products, which produce new profits. The more you can learn about the quality of a company's management, the better your investment decisions will be.

B. Knowledge of competitors' management. Companies do not exist in a vacuum, and neither does corporate decision-making. You need to know whether your company is a leader or a follower, whether its management makes better or poorer decisions than its competitors. Where your company stands among its peers is generally, though not always, a measure of how well your company's management stacks up.

C. Wall Street analysts. The real function of Wall Street analysts is to act as soothsayers. They look at the information on a company's balance sheet, add in their knowledge of the marketplace and the economy, and develop a model of future earnings. The discounted future-earnings model that every analyst uses forms the basis of the market multiple; the premium the stock market is willing to pay in now for a hopefully growing stream of future earnings. What you know about the analysts who follow your company, and the quality of their forecasts, can help you make better investment decisions.

D. Macroeconomic information. Every quarter, companies and governments release reams of data about the performance of the company, its industry, and the economy in which it functions. Analysts use this data to adjust their models and to upgrade or downgrade stocks. If the economy begins to flag, stocks go down because future earnings prospects are going to dim, lowering the premium—the multiple—which people are willing to pay for those earnings. If the economy remains strong, the multiple holds steady or it continues to rise.

Every investor needs to make use of all this knowledge. The better you understand it and know how to use it, the more likely that you will do well as an investor in stocks. It's that simple.

As a prelude to explaining the marketplace-check system, I'll put it into the context of the other four information sources you must have to invest. What follows has nothing to do with marketplace checks per se. But all information is acquired in similar ways, so if you learn how to seek out and interpret information about the other components, you'll have a pretty fair head start on setting up a marketplace-check system. Also, because you're not a Wall Street professional with millions of dollars to invest, you're not going to get the best information from these other critical information sources unless you go after them yourself.

After I explain how to get the information, we'll examine the pros and cons of each of these sources, and I'll show you how to use each to its best advantage.

Since you will be collecting a lot of information on companies, you'd best begin by setting up a filing system for your information. As most small investors have limited resources, you probably will be investing in no more than a dozen companies. Go out and buy a dozen accordion folders (the stiff brown manila type that lawyers use, which expand to hold lots of documents). Put a stick-on label on each folder. If you already have a portfolio of stocks, write the name of one company on each folder. You will place press clippings, notes, printed reports, and other paper documents into these folders. At the same time, set up corresponding folders on the hard drive of your computer. This will contain information more easily stored electronically. Taking clippings off the Internet, or E-mails from sources and putting them in your computer folders is extremely efficient. I recommend that everyone become as computer literate as possible. I attended school when term papers were written on manual typewriters, so the joys of drag and drop are endless. However, if you want to stick only to the accordion folders, that system works perfectly well. Now you are ready to begin gathering the basic information that you'll need to make better decisions.

Let's examine each in turn.

A. Company management. Companies are really just large collections of people working together for a common goal under the leadership of an executive team. What you can learn about the people who run a company is of absolute importance in helping you make investment decisions. But where do you learn about company management? Most business-magazine stories praise good management teams and leaders far too much, and are far too critical about management they consider weak or poor. As Roger Smith, the former CEO of General Motors, once noted, he was never as bad as reporters made him out to be when he was being vilified, and never as good as when he was being praised.

Where do you go to learn about company management? The company's Web site will give you a basic idea of what the company does, and how it fits into the marketplace. (Remember: This is the information the company wants you to know.) Once you have gone through the Web site, you can call up the public-affairs (investor relations) department and ask them for any additional information that you feel is missing. That might be biographies of the current management team, as well as a biography of the previous chief executive if the current CEO has been running the company for less than five years.

Why do you need the old CEO's biography? Because unless the company was sold, or unless it has remade itself completely, many of the policies of the prior CEO will still be in place. You need to know as much about that person's thinking and temperament as you do about the current group of corporate officers.

When you are examining corporate biographies, the first thing to look for is what they *did,* rather than what they do now. If you see that many of the corporate officers have marketing backgrounds, you can make a good guess that you are dealing with a marketing-driven company. The benefit is that the senior management has its eye on making sales grow. A potential down side of being marketing-heavy is that the company may be neglecting its research and day-to-day operations. If, on the other hand, you see that a company is heavy with finance types, you can assume that a lot of attention is being paid to costs, and marketing is less important.

For an example of how management shapes companies, let's look at the U.S. automobile industry. Since the 1960s, the automakers have had very distinct personalities, and these have been reflected almost perfectly in who rises to the top. For starters, examine General Motors. Since the 1960s, nearly every CEO of General Motors has come out of the finance side of the company, and has spent a large portion of his career at the General Motors building in New York, rather than being immersed in the auto culture of Detroit. They know an awful lot about how cars are financed, and about capital spending and pension plans and all of the other things that go into figuring out the cost equation of making automobiles; but they often know very little about cars, and tend to leave the details to the marketing people, who rarely have the ear of top management.

Ford CEOs are efficiency experts. Starting more than fifty years ago, when Robert S. McNamara was at Ford, the company developed cadres of managers who know how to wring every penny out of the production department. Ford is the most international of the automobile companies, and it has used its global know-how to source parts all over the world, and to develop common platforms which allow cars made in different nations to use the same parts. As a result, Ford can make cars for less money than any other U.S. car company.

Until it merged with Daimler-Benz a few years ago, Chrysler was a company run by marketing people and "car guys," engineers and stylists with a love of engines and sheet metal, and their cars reflected it. The company wasn't very good on financial controls, so it got itself into deep trouble in the 1970s and again in the 1980s. It wasn't until the late 1980s, when it found the right combination of finance people and car people that the company really hit its stride, turning out well-designed, good-quality autos at a reasonable price.

As you can see, each company mirrored the skills of its management. This is true for almost every company, so it really does pay to know something about the backgrounds of the CEOs and senior executives who run the show.

Next, look at where the managers went to school. It sounds strange, but where you went to school is more important than what you learned. That's because schools provide the foundation of networking. For example, I went to Lehigh University for my undergraduate degree and to Yale for my master's degree in management. As a result, several of the key people I've recruited over the years have come from one or the other of those schools. Company management works the same way. When a CEO has a problem that he can't solve inside the company, he's likely to call up the alumni office of his school to find out what a former respected classmate is doing. When a new CEO comes into the company from outside, you know that he's going to bring in a bunch of people with whom he feels comfortable, and that means people from his old school and his old company. For example, when Lee Iacocca left Ford to go to Chrysler in the early 1970s, he brought so many people with him that they were known collectively as the "Gang of Ford." When you see domination of a company by a small group of like-minded or similarly educated people, you have to be able to figure out what it means.

Often, it means two things. First, if the new CEO has a good reputation as a leader, he is probably going to bring a lot of good people with him, and that is going to be beneficial to the company you are analyzing. But he is also going to take people away from the company he has just left, and those people take their knowledge and their skills, which cannot be replaced easily. Arno Penzias, who is a Nobel Prize–winning physicist who ran Bell Labs for awhile, asserts that in any given field, there are only about five people who are the real innovators and have most of the critical skills; so if you move them from one company to another, you are not only adding to one side, but definitely subtracting from the other side.

Once you have gone through the company supplied biographies, it's time to look at other sources of information. The Internet is a good place to look. Find out the company's headquarters and look up the name of the CEO and the other top officers of the company in the files of the local newspaper, which are increasingly on the World Wide Web.

You might find some things that surprise you. You might find that an esteemed CEO has been arrested for drunk driving, or that he has been involved in a messy divorce, or that he has invested in a side business which has done poorly. CEOs are public figures, so reporters go after them the same way that they go after celebrities, cataloging their every move, always on the alert for a headline-grabbing misstep. What they learn and report is valuable to you because it helps you get a better handle on the quality of management's judgment and decision-making skills. Chances are, if they are making good decisions in their personal lives, they are making sound decisions in their business life, and vice versa.

Now that you have compiled an impressive dossier of information on the management of the companies you've chosen, it's time to put it to work. Get out the annual report of the company, which should be one of those items you have in your accordion folder. (It will come to you once a year, along with your voting proxies. Save the annual report, as well as the quarterly reports. Do not throw out old reports as new ones come in. You'll need a couple of years' worth in order to begin making meaningful comparisons later on.) You want to look at just a couple of items on the consolidated balance sheet, and you want to look at one or two other things in the annual report.

First, look at sales. Are they rising and, if so, by what percentage? Then examine profits, and then at general, sales, and administrative (GS&A) expenses. Let's look at Acme Widget, a hypothetical company, and see how these numbers reveal a lot about the quality of management.

**Acme Widget
Income Statement**

	2000	1999
Total Revenues	$6,065,809	$5,439,554
Cost of Goods Sold	4,118,906	3,700,428
Gross Profit	1,947,713	1,739,126
Selling, General and Administrative	$1,663,326	$1,502,426
Net Income	$ 284,387	$ 236,700

Now we can make some simple calculations. Sales rose 11.5 percent in 2000 over 1999, a nice double-digit increase. Net income rose 20.1 percent in the same period, which is an extremely good increase. Selling expenses rose 10.7 percent.

Now let's look at the numbers a little differently. In 2000, net income was 4.7 percent of sales, compared to 4.4 percent in 1999. Selling expenses were 27.4 percent of sales in 2000, compared to 27.6 percent in 1999.

What does all this tell us about the company and its management? Plenty. Almost anytime a company can increase its sales by more than 10 percent year over year, it is doing something right; and if it can increase profits by more than 20 percent year over year, management is especially to be commended for being on the ball.

From these numbers, we can tell that Acme probably has some hot products that are in strong demand, and that the management is working as hard as it can to sell those products. We can infer that from the cost of selling, which rose slightly. Acme was putting more money behind its products in an effort to persuade customers to buy more, and it obviously paid off because net income rose by more than 20 percent.

On the other hand, whenever selling costs rise much above 20 percent, that is a danger signal. It can mean that the market is extremely crowded and competitive, and that Acme has to do a lot of price discounting in order to persuade customers to buy its products over a competitor's. We know that this is true because Acme's net-income margin as a percentage of sales is low, less than 5 percent. Net margins that are low tell you that the business is very competitive. The lower the number, the more competitive, and the more commoditylike the product is likely to be (that is, the fewer competitive advantages that customers can discern for themselves).

Overall, these few numbers tell us that Acme's management is working hard in a tough competitive environment to sell more of its products, and it is succeeding, because of the large jump in net income.

Summarize these numbers, on a piece of paper, just like the example above, and put it into your folder. When you get to the next step—competitive management—you're going to do the same thing for each of the companies that competes within your industry, so you'll know just how well your company is doing vis-à-vis its competition. This is where having your files on your computer will really help. If you put this information on a spreadsheet (like Excel or Lotus1-2-3) you will be able to compare and manipulate the figures with speed, accuracy, and even pleasure.

Now extract one more bit of information from the annual report. Go into the section titled "Management Discussion" and read the section on new products. New products and services are the lifeblood of a company. Ideally, a company should get at least one-third of its revenue from products whose life cycle is less than five years old. If there is a lot of discussion about new products, that is a good sign. If there isn't, learn to be skeptical about the company's future.

Now that you have a pretty good picture of how well the company treats its shareholders—the better the profit picture, the better you are being treated—you want to know how well management treats itself. Information about how much money the management team earns, and what kinds of incentives they have given themselves in stock options and bonuses can be found in two forms that must be filed with the Securities and Exchange Commission. These are forms 10-K and 10-Q, and you can get both from the company just by asking for them. Better yet, go to the SEC Web site (www.sec.gov). It is very well organized and easy to use. You should go the section marked EDGAR. That is the SEC's database. If you have Adobe's Acrobat Reader (which can be downloaded from the Web for free) you can read, store and print the PDFs (Portable Document Format) from your computer. These look identical to the printed forms and filings. The 10-K discloses not only salaries and bonuses and stock-option plans, but it also tells you how well the company is doing versus its competitors and versus the common indices. A couple of years ago, the SEC forced companies to put a small chart into its 10-K, so that investors could see at a glance how well their company's management was doing compared to managers in similar companies. The chart shows the rise or fall of all stocks within an industry; so if you pick up Procter & Gamble's 10-K, you'll see a little chart comparing its performance to Colgate-Palmolive, Johnson & Johnson, and Clorox. Of course, management will spend a lot of time telling you why the comparison isn't really meaningful; but as a starting point, it is quite useful, especially if your stock is lagging and your managers are paying themselves very high salaries. If they are, you probably want to put your money elsewhere.

B. Competitors' management. The 10-K list of competitors shows which companies the SEC believes are the legitimate competition for the company in which you have invested. The SEC picks not only companies in the same field, with the same products, but also companies of comparable size. For starters, that is probably good enough; but as you get better at doing this kind of research, you'll probably want to buy yourself a copy of *Hoover's*

Handbook of American Business (or find it on the Internet). Hoover's lists all of a company's competitors, big and small, at the end of each company profile. Why is that important? Later on, as we're doing our marketplace checks, you'll notice that smaller companies often come into an existing marketplace and do very well, introducing new products that larger companies later either acquire or imitate. For example, for years there was a product called Softsoap, made by the Minnetonka Soap Company in Minnesota. Its share of the hand-soap market kept rising, year after year, until one day, Colgate-Palmolive up and bought the company. Minnetonka Soap would never have shown up as a competitor of Colgate's—yet it was, in at least one important product line. Learn to look for companies like Minnetonka because, when you're doing marketplace checks, that's where a lot of the real investing upside comes from.

Minnetonka is a good example because it shows you the differences among competitors. A company that introduces interesting new products can change the face of a market rapidly. Look at television. For about twenty years, analysts have talked about the rising impact of cable programming on the viability of network television's Big Three. So when Fox started its own network, many people believed it would fail because they thought that the battle was between the networks and the cable channels. In hindsight, the fact that ABC, CBS, and NBC were distracted by cable allowed the Fox network the time it needed to find an audience. As a result, there are now not three, but six networks. As 2001 began, the Big Three networks not only had to compete with the highly fractured field of cable channels, but also against alternative broad audience-based networks, like Fox, UPN, and WB.

Evaluating the competition is critical to knowing whether a company has the staying power to justify the multiple on discounted future earnings that Wall Street is going to assign it. You could be looking at the best local retailer on the planet, but how well will it endure once Wal-Mart invades its category? Toys R Us is the classic example. Wal-Mart grabbed off so much of the toy market so quickly—15 percent in only three years—that it sent Toys R Us into a frenzy of worry, right after the company's founder, Charles Lazarus, retired in 1994. Wal-Mart began to aggressively offer the hottest-selling toys at lower prices, and upscale stores began siphoning off the high-profit end of the business. Toys R Us's new management was spending so much time worrying about those threats that it completely failed to notice the rise of the Internet, and the emergence of brand-new competitors.

When you evaluate management, you are really making a judgment about how well they can persevere when the going gets tough. You are looking at the management of the company in which you have invested, and at its competitors, and asking a simple question: "Who is smarter?" To find out, don't just look at the stock prices. Go back to the brief sheet you made for each company. Now you're going to turn it into a little table. As an example, I'm going to use four consumer-products companies: Procter & Gamble, Colgate-Palmolive, Johnson & Johnson, and Clorox. We're going to look at several years' worth of performance, from 1990 through 1994. First we'll look at sales, then earnings. (We'll forget about selling costs, because these are very high for each of the companies.)

	1990	1991	1992	1993	1994
Sales					
P&G	$24,081	$27,026	$29,362	$30,433	$33,434
Colgate	5,691	6,060	7,007	7,141	7,588
Clorox	1,484	1,647	1,717	1,634	1,837
J&J	11,232	12,447	13,753	14,138	15,734
Percent Gain					
P&G		12.23%	8.64%	3.64%	9.86%
Colgate		6.48	10.00	1.91	6.25

	1990	1991	1992	1993	1994
Clorox		10.98	4.25	−1.95	12.42
J&J		10.82	10.49	2.80	11.29
Net Profits					
P&G	$ 1,602	$ 1,773	$ 1,872	$ 269	$ 2,211
Colgate	321	125	477	548	580
Clorox	154	53	118	167	212
J&J	1,143	1,461	1,625	1,787	2,006
Percent Gain					
P&G		10.67%	5.58%	−85.6%	622%
Colgate		−61.1	181.6	14.88	5.84
Clorox		−65.5	122.6	41.5	26.95
J&J		27.82	11.22	9.96	12.25
Profit/Sales					
P&G	.066%	.066%	.064%	.008%	.066%
Colgate	.056	.021	.068	.077	.076
Clorox	.104	.032	.069	.102	.115
J&J	.101	.117	.118	.126	.127

Whose management was best over time? Clearly it was Johnson & Johnson. While all the manufacturers' sales and profits went up and down during the period, only J&J managed to increase the ratio of profits to sales every year. That means the company used some combination of more new products and better control of expense to increase sales and profits at the same time. None of the other companies in the group was as successful.

Yet, whose stock performed worst over that same period? You guessed it. Johnson & Johnson's shares barely doubled between 1990 and 1994, while shares of Colgate rose 161 percent, and P&G's and Clorox's shares both rose about 110 percent. Here is a great example of how Wall Street often misreads information, and consequently creates opportunities.

Such discrepancies of information never exist forever. By 1995, relative prices of shares of J&J had begun to rocket past those of its competitors. By September 2000, shares of J&J had risen 150 percent further. Clorox's shares rose about 85 percent, Procter & Gamble's about 50 percent and Colgate 120 percent.

When you run simple numbers like these—all done with just a calculator—you get to see the relative efforts of management reflected in the harsh reality of the results. When you make your investment decisions, knowing that a particular management is doing a consistently better job than its competitors is reason enough to invest, even if Wall Street is ignoring the information. At some point, everyone else will catch on.

C. Wall Street analysts. This, of course, brings us to the next issue. Wall Street analysts do not, in fact, always catch on. When it comes to financial research, most people immediately conjure up the analysts they see on CNBC and CNN/FN. These are the people who crank out the numbers, who read the financial statements, who visit with the chief financial officers of the companies they track, and who make the predictions upon which investors make their decisions. If an analyst raises his or her estimates by a couple of cents, investors rush to their telephones and computer screens and buy more stock. If the analyst says that Acme Widget is not going to meet his numbers, the stock generally falls.

This type of information is extremely valuable, but the numbers generated by the analysts have a seeming absoluteness that either intimidates investors or lulls them into a false sense of security. But what investors don't know about Wall Street analysis can kill them. Wall Street analysis has been around in some form almost as long as Wall Street has. The idea of assigning a risk rating—that is really what an analyst's "Buy" or "Sell" decision actually is—goes all the way back to the Lloyd's coffeehouse in London, and the assigning of insurance risks to sailing ships. For as long as stocks have traded, people have written about the prospects of the companies behind them; but it wasn't until the Great Depression that the role of analyst began to be taken seriously. Before then, analysts were considered as little more than racetrack touts, shilling the stocks of the companies that brokers were attempting to sell. But during the Great Depression and immediately after it, brokerage firms, especially Merrill Lynch, began to professionalize the role of analyst, in the hopes that investors would take the information given to them by independent-minded analysts and use it as the basis of their stock purchases.

For about five decades, that formula worked, and investors returned to the stock markets slowly but steadily. But just as investing became as commonplace as it had in the 1920s, the analysts' role began to change, and the information they began to produce began to change as well. In the great wave of brokerage-house consolidation that began in the 1970s and continues today, brokerages began to expand the investment-banking relationships they had with the companies they were covering. The role of the analyst shifted suddenly from neutral arbiter to originator of investment-banking deals—uncovering the next merger candidate, the next takeover target—for a yet larger investment-banking client of the firm.

Ironically, individual investors first noticed this when it already was too late. In the 1970s, *Institutional Investor* magazine began to nominate its "all-American Research Team," and ordinary investors suddenly thought they had a new tool available to them. Most people thought that becoming an *I.I.* all-American meant that an analyst's research was really sound. Mostly, it really meant that the analyst chosen was especially good at telling his or her institutional clients about breaking merger activity, or bringing merger and takeover deals to his or her firm. It had very little to do with actually being able to crunch numbers, or being able to predict the rise and fall of individual stocks accurately.

Today, this is even truer. The "best" analysts are those who are able to bring Internet IPOs to their firms, people such as Mary Meeker of Morgan Stanley Dean Witter or Henry Blodget of Merrill Lynch, and earn their firms huge underwriting fees in the process. Most analysts, when they actually do crunch numbers, increasingly do so with the guidance of the chief financial officers of the companies they cover. Company CFOs increasingly "manage" their earnings to make them conform to the consensus of the analysts who cover the company. This creates a very dangerous situation for the average investor, but it also creates enormous opportunity because, in the process of managing expectations, huge information discrepancies, such as the one I showed you earlier—Procter & Gamble versus Johnson & Johnson—open up.

So how do you get the truth from analysts? First, there are a couple of different kinds of analysts. There are big-company analysts and small-company analysts, and there are buy-side and sell-side analysts. The big-company analysts are the people who work for the huge Wall Street firms like Merrill Lynch, Morgan Stanley Dean Witter, J.P. Morgan, Chase & Co., Goldman Sachs, PaineWebber, and Prudential Securities. The primary business of all these firms is investment banking, and they do retail brokerage on the side to gain access to your money, which goes into the pool and increases the leverage they can offer in each successive investment-banking deal. This does not mean that these companies don't have your interests at heart. They are all uniformly well managed and, with a couple of exceptions—the odd hiccup—they protect investors well, and sometimes even do well by the people who invest with them. But when you are investing with these brokers, remember that they manage their own interests better than they manage yours. That's how they make their own profits.

Smaller brokerages, especially regional brokers, often do a better job on behalf of investors. Regional brokerages often provide much better in-depth coverage of companies in their region because they are likely to have local contacts with the CEO and CFO of the company, rather than having to fly in and establish a relationship. Outside of New York, the elite in any given city is smaller, and people who run things or pay attention to who is running them all tend to belong to the same clubs and send their kids to the same schools. So when you are doing investment research and looking at analysts, get yourself a copy of *Nelson's Directory of Investment Research,* which is the bible of company researchers, and look up the companies you own. See who are the big-brokerage analysts, and look to find out who are the regional ones. If you find a regional analyst in the same location as the company in which you are interested—the Robinson-Humphrey analyst for Scientific-Atlanta, say—that's the person to call for an opinion. Good financial writers know this, so when you are reading *Forbes* or *Fortune* or *The Wall Street Journal* or *Investor's Business Daily,* or any of several other publications, always check who the writer is quoting. If it's a local analyst, chances are he or she is very knowledgeable.

While it can pay off, putting your faith in a regional brokerage does have some obstacles. Take, for example, the infamous case of Janney Montgomery Scott and its casino analyst, Marvin Roffman. In 1990, Roffman correctly predicted that the bonds of Donald Trump's Taj Mahal Casino were significantly overvalued. Janney Montgomery Scott is headquartered in Philadelphia and the casino was just down the expressway in Atlantic City, so Roffman had the opportunity to do the best kind of marketplace check there was: He heard a rumor, and went down and hung around the casino, counting the daily attendance and watching how many people were playing the dollar slot machines. His conclusions, written in a devastating report, caused shudders on Wall Street because many big banks had loaned Trump a large fortune. Trump protested, and Roffman's firm, which was also heavily invested in Trump, pressured him to change his report. When he refused, they fired him. When Roffman turned out to be right, he looked like a hero—but Janney didn't hire him back.

There is yet another divide in analysts that you ought to know about. That's buy-side and sell-side. Analysts who work for the brokerage houses are called sell-side analysts because they are backing up the sales forces of these companies, the retail brokers. Sell-side analysts not only have investment-banking conflicts of interest, they have selling pressures on them as well. When a large brokerage house that has just floated an initial public offering puts out its first report on the new company, the rating is almost always "Buy" because the company's brokers are attempting to sell the stock they have committed to selling. That's just the way things work. It isn't dishonest or unethical, but it *does* mean that you have to take the analyst's word with a grain of salt.

Buy-side analysts are analysts who work for the large institutions that buy and hold stocks for other people. Peter Lynch, the hugely popular public face of Fidelity Investments, was a buy-side analyst who became the head of the company's enormously successful Magellan Fund. People on the buy side are paid to be skeptical because their performance is going to be based on how well their purchases perform. Buy-side analysts are largely invisible, but there are ways to track their movements. All mutual fund managers employ teams of buy-side analysts. It is a simple task to get yourself a copy of Morningstar's analysis of mutual fund holdings, and then buy the same stocks that the top-performing funds buy. Since you probably don't have enough money to buy all of them, buy the top five or ten stocks in the portfolios of the top managers. It's a really simple way to stay on top of the market. Moreover, if you track one manager carefully, you'll begin to learn to think more along the lines of the manager, which can't hurt.

D. Macroeconomic information. Shrewd analysts pay a lot of attention to what is going on in the economy at large because the economy gives them clues about what is going to happen to products in companies they follow. For example, if sales of McDonald's hamburgers go up, that means that more cows are being slaughtered. More cows mean that farmers need to buy more grain to fatten them, and that more cattle cars are going to be needed to transport the cows from the ranches to the feedlots, and then from the feedlots to the slaughterhouses. It also means that there will be more cowhides available for leather. So, in simple terms, a rise in McDonald's also means a rise in feed prices, a rise in railcar usage, higher utilization and more overtime at the slaughterhouses, and cheaper leather for shoes, handbags, and furniture.

But in our highly competitive society, for every winner there is a loser, so it also probably means falling chicken consumption, and falling prices for competing fabric coverings. Every economic event is like a ripple in a very large lake, and it is the business of business economists to interpret these ripples. Several decades ago, Lawrence Klein, of the University of Pennsylvania's Wharton School of Business, took all of these ripples and figured out more or less how they related to each other and developed something he called the input/output model of economics. He won a Nobel Prize for his work. Economists now know that the economy is much more complex than the models Klein developed, but input/output theory is still an important way of looking at the economy.

As an investor, you have to look at things much the same way. In fact, when you begin doing marketplace checks, you're asking the fundamental input/output question: Who is helped and who is hurt by any given activity? If you go to your local drugstore and you see that they've expanded the candy aisle, it was at the expense of something else in the store, because the store has a fixed amount of space. If you go to the same store often enough, you'll notice what is selling and what isn't, what categories are getting more shelf space and which are getting less, and you'll have a pretty good local-level input/output model, which is a perfect place to begin marketplace checks.

The same thing works at the macro level. Events happen, many of which a company's management does not know how to anticipate. Your favorite company is in the business of exporting its product to Southeast Asia, and the Asian economy goes into the tank. Nobody expected it, but suddenly sales begin to fall and even the best management is going to have a difficult time coping with the situation. Good management maintains contingency plans, and reacts quickly. So should smart investors.

4

How I Became a
Marketplace Checker

I wish I could say that marketplace checks were original with me, but they aren't. Good reporters and good analysts have been doing marketplace checks through all of recorded history. When Moses sent Joshua into the land of Canaan, he was doing a marketplace check. When Marco Polo and his father went to China, they were doing a marketplace check. But even if I can't take credit for inventing marketplace checks, I can say that most of my life—and practically all of my career—has been spent in learning to be a good marketplace checker. My life has taken all sorts of interesting twists, and I've probably started more than the average number of businesses. But every one of those business start-ups—both the successful ones and the failures— taught me lessons that have been effective in marketplace checking. In fact, the things you need to do to get a new business off the ground—the research, the market analysis, the questioning of ideas—are the very things that make marketplace checking work.

What starts you out in marketplace checking for investing purposes is exactly what starts you out when you create a new business. You have to want to make money. That's what started me going. The fundamental desire to make and have money, which I have had since I was a kid, is what helped turn me into a marketplace checker. And while I'm reasonably intelligent, it wasn't brains that made me successful at what I'm doing. It was more a kind of happenstance, with a bit of luck thrown in, coupled with a lot of hard work.

Here's my story. I was one of those kids who always wanted to have a little more money than I received as allowance. You know the kind of kid I'm talking about. They're the ones who open lemonade stands in the summer and shovel driveways for a couple of dollars in the winter. When they get older, they mow lawns and deliver papers, and pick up bottles and cans to redeem them for the deposit. Some of those kids go on to become real eager-beaver types. Ross Johnson, the former CEO of RJR Nabisco, was the kind of go-getter I'm talking about. He started out delivering newspapers as a kid in western Canada, and began a lifelong career of selling that finally led him to Nabisco's executive suite. My earliest endeavors were similar. I was always looking for ways to make extra money, but my desire for extra cash was tempered by the desire to not work too hard. I wanted to play baseball, and that was more important than making money. I wanted to be with my friends and have a few bucks in my pocket, and I'd work just hard enough to reach that immediate goal.

My early life was going along like that—earn a little and spend it—until everything changed with the death of my father. In the early 1970s he had been the CFO of a NYSE-listed corporation. In a downsizing reorganization, he lost his job, and very soon afterward died of a heart attack. This single event affected almost every part of my life, as it does any youngster. Losing a parent when you are a child teaches you that life is not fair, and that events are often random, irrational. Losing a parent forces you to accept the mortality of those you love, and your own mortality as well. In time, losing a parent or any loved one teaches you to value everything in life. But it also teaches you that absolutely nothing is secure. And in the early days it taught me the importance of real financial security, which is not—as most people think—a steady paycheck. Real financial security is having sufficient money so that if you didn't work every day, you could still live reasonably well. That's what my father's death taught me, and I decided that I was going to become a financially independent person as rapidly as I could.

That meant starting my own business instead of working for an existing business. In the 1970s, magazines like *Free Enterprise, Inc.,* and *Success* were telling people that if you could find a business that provided a unique product or service that was not already sold in your area, you could make money, because you would have no competition. That's an almost quaint idea nowadays, with so many well-established business categories. But you have to remember that the early 1970s were the period when we finally shook off the conservatism of the Depression era, and began to look at the world as a place of opportunity rather than of limits. All of this fit me to a T. In the early 1970s I was a man in a hurry. Not only did I want success, I wanted it *now.*

Sitting in my fraternity-house room at Lehigh University, in Bethlehem, Pennsylvania, I began to try to figure out what a good business might be. That meant looking for something that was missing. Looking for something that is missing is a skill that can be learned. It takes practice. Sometimes what happens is that 90 percent of the puzzle is there, and you just have to fill in the last piece. That's how I developed my first real business. One rainy evening, I decided to get some pizza. On my way out, a guy down the hall asked if I would pick up one for him. I said yes, and he handed over the $6 for a $5.50 pie. "I don't have change," he said. "Keep the 50 cents for gas."

Thinking nothing of it, I went off, having done a good deed. Over that semester, being one of the few students on campus with a car, I was making quite a few runs for pizza. You have to understand that while Lehigh was right in town, it sat pretty far up a very steep hill from Fourth Street, where the nearest restaurants are. Nobody would willingly go down the hill without a sure way to get back up. So, suddenly, when my fraternity brothers found out that I was making pizza runs, I wound up picking up five or six pizzas on each trip. It was becoming a pain, and I was feeling a bit put out. One very rainy night, I arrived at the pizza place and complained to the owner that I was sick and tired of being everyone's delivery boy for gas money. The pizzeria owner said he would gladly pay 50 cents for each pizza I delivered.

Suddenly an inconvenience became an opportunity.

With the excitement that only a group of college sophomores can generate, I gathered a few friends, plastered the campus with flyers, and waited for the orders to come in. As is so often the case with a really good idea, the problem is not getting customers, but controlling growth. We were flooded with orders. We didn't have our logistics set up. We didn't know how to handle calls, or how to schedule deliveries. Instead, we just tried to take every order we could. It took a tremendous amount of work, and I was just not prepared to do all the organization and structuring work required for any successful operation. We earned enough money for a fabulous spring break, but when we returned, with baseball in the air, I decided not to pursue the business. From this experience, I learned one of the cardinal rules of business: If you want to do something entrepreneurial, which requires your heart and your soul, you had better love the business you are in. At eighty hours a week, money alone is not enough motivation.

With me out of the picture, the pizza parlor owner started his own delivery service for the students of Lehigh University, and it became quite successful. Unbeknownst to me, two students from the University of Michigan, Tom and James

Monaghan, had the same idea back in 1960. They not only worked hard, but they clearly loved their work. Their company became Domino's Pizza.

A few years later found me in graduate business school at Yale. There I was exposed to the latest theories on marketing, economics, finance, organizational behavior, and a host of other academic practices that were supposed to prepare me to run corporations of any size or description. While I was at Yale, I became an avid magazine reader. It didn't matter what the magazine was. If it was around, I read it. And that's where I discovered an interesting fact: All the best ideas aren't in the big-circulation business magazines. In fact, if you read about a "hot" company or product or service in *Forbes, Fortune,* or *Business Week,* it's no longer a hot company or product or service. All the best ideas are in trade magazines and special-interest publications, which the general public rarely sees. If you read about a really neat restaurant concept in *Restaurant News,* you may still be ahead of the crowd. But once it is featured in *Business Week,* everyone knows about it. It's one of those things to keep in mind for later, when you begin to do your own marketplace checking.

While I was in graduate school, I read a number of articles from different publications that all basically said the same thing: People were spending a lot of money on their pets. I also read a few articles that talked about an increased interest in art, a few that spoke of a rise in horse ownership, and still others that talked about a trend in decorating toward personal mementos, rather than standardized items.

I put these four trends together and came up with the notion that you could make money by offering horse owners custom portraits of their horses. Since I was no longer a shallow undergraduate, but now a smart B-school student, I didn't just run with the idea. I did some work on the feasibility of this business. I learned that I could buy mailing lists of horse owners, and that it was possible to rent a booth at horse shows. I even found a company that could produce the oils at a very reasonable cost. I came up with a price that would ensure me a great deal of profit. I used all the skills I had learned at business school, ran all the numbers, and was getting set to launch.

Just before the launch, I was visiting my then-girlfriend's house. She owned a horse, and as I walked into the family's living room, my heart soared. There above the fireplace was an oil portrait of my girlfriend's horse. What more evidence did I need? I excitedly explained my surefire plan to my girlfriend's mother. She looked at me and said, "It won't work." I heard what she said, but figured she just didn't understand. I explained it again, listing all the market trends that I had discovered, and pointing out that she herself had a horse portrait in her own living room. She laughed. "Oh, that," she said, "Our neighbor painted it. It's nice, but no one I know would actually buy a portrait, especially at your prices."

I discounted her comments as the meaningless talk of a New Jersey housewife. I went ahead with my plan. I sent out 15,000 letters and received not one single response. What had gone wrong? I had overintellectualized the concept and violated a fundamental rule of business: I did not listen to my customer base.

Business magazines and newspapers like *The Wall Street Journal* will happily tell you about the business visionaries who went against the conventional wisdom, broke all the rules, and succeeded despite all the odds. Those are stories that are supposed to inspire entrepreneurs and make them want to carry on against all hope. It's not that such stories are not true. They often are. Fred Smith really *did* start FedEx based on a business plan that was given a mediocre grade in graduate school. Sam Walton really *did* quit his job at the Ben Franklin stores and open his first Wal-Mart in a poor rural town in Arkansas. Ben Cohen and Jerry Greenfield really did buy an ice-cream formula from Penn State University for $5 and used it to start a company that changed the face of frozen desserts.

If you want to use those stories to inspire you to hold on to your vision, that's fine. But the fact remains that 99 percent of the time, the conventional wisdom—that most businesses fail, and that most ideas do not succeed in the marketplace—is correct.

I learned from all these setbacks, and much of what I learned helped to make me not only a successful businessman, but ultimately, a successful marketplace checker.

You see, many of the skills needed to start a business are the same skills needed to do marketplace checking. You have to research a business idea thoroughly. You have to know what other companies are doing. You have to learn to be skeptical of your own insights, and to always accumulate more information. And you have to learn how to trust your judgment when the time is right.

I learned all this from starting businesses, and I learned most of them while I was making mistakes. Indeed, there's a lot of truth in the old adage that you learn more from your mistakes than from your successes. When you are successful, there are generally a great many factors that contribute to the overall outcome. Most of us would like to assume that our success is due primarily to our own brilliance and hard work, and leave it at that. After all, why raise questions when the money is rolling in? There is a business to run, and lots of other things to occupy your attention. But when things go wrong, you need to analyze every decision, and if you can maintain your objectivity, you can usually isolate the critical areas of trouble. You remember and avoid them in the future. Eventually, you get it right.

After I finished at Yale, I moved to California. I went into advertising and began to teach marketing. During this period, I stayed current with the latest academic trends and, thanks to hundreds of inquisitive students, I kept on top of consumer trends as well. In my spare time, I created several ventures. Some were very successful. One in particular was corporate seminars, where I organized a week's worth of training for mid-management. I would cover the basic concepts of finance, accounting, marketing, and organizational behavior. A sort of forty-hour MBA. Corporate HR departments were very receptive, as my seminars provided an effective training in management. I gave up this business only as my other commitments grew and I had to make decisions to let go of successful ventures to concentrate on *very* successful ventures.

Eventually, I had to let go of them all to concentrate on my *best* venture: marketplace checks. It is hard to let go of a business that is going well, and makes you money. But I have also found that if you spread yourself too thin, then everything starts to deteriorate just a bit. You can keep it together for quite some time, but eventually the volume of work overtakes you. Besides, if you're going to be successful, you have to make time to relax and think. You can't be open to the next great idea if your nose is always buried in your business.

I'll tell you one last story of an idea that was successful, but still failed. As a person who subscribes to and reads more than fifty magazines, I was being deluged by junk mail, dozens of solicitations and catalogs every day. It got to the point that I couldn't go off for a long weekend without returning to an overflowing mailbox. I spoke to many people who said that junk mail was becoming a real problem and that they would gladly pay to have it stopped. I did some checking and knew I had a customer base that would pay for the service.

Thus, my next company, Junk Mail Busters, was born. The idea was simple: For a small fee, people could send us their junk-mail labels and we'd have their names removed from the junk-mail lists. Since I had removed my name from many mailing lists and had reduced my mail considerably, I knew that the service could be provided.

At least, I thought I knew. I put an ad in several activist magazines, and almost at once I was flooded with subscribers to my service. As I had assumed, a great many people were on multiple lists. Therefore, it was a relatively easy task to send one letter with dozens of names. This concept looked pretty good. I was providing a service that people wanted, and I was going to make some money doing it.

But I had not done my research. The direct-mail industry struck back. I received a letter from the industry's organization which said that only persons whose names were on the list could request that their names be removed. They would not accept letters with multiple requests. This totally destroyed the economics of my business. I faced a dilemma. I could have sued the direct-mail industry organization, or I could have returned the fees to the individuals and instructed them how to remove their names from the lists.

I chose the latter.

The lesson here was that even if the overall concept of a business is correct, make sure you are not tripped up by seemingly peripheral issues. In this case, I should have researched the legal issues. When you are doing marketplace checks, you will find that the idea of paying attention to peripheral issues can pay off.

Take the recent example of Ford and Firestone/Bridgestone. Ford has spent billions of dollars making itself into a highly profitable global car company, buying such upscale brands as Jaguar to increase its overall profitability. When the story about Firestone's defective tires first broke, everyone believed that it was a tire story. But a savvy marketplace checker would have asked a simple question: "Why did Firestone's tires fail on so many Ford SUVs?" The answer, which may never be known, is less important than the consequences: Despite Ford CEO Jacques Nasser's assurances, consumers became suspicious of Ford's products, which sent the stock tumbling.

The trick in life is to learn from all of your experiences. Over the past thirty years, I've been involved with many business ventures—some successful and some less so—but I learned something from each one of them. *The most important thing I learned was to be more observant, and to listen to what people are saying, not for what you want to hear.* Almost as important is involvement with activities that interest you. That goes for the industries and companies that you research and in which you invest. *You'll find that if you are really knowledgeable about an industry which makes you passionate, you have a chance to make as much money as the smartest investor in the highest-flying high-technology stocks.*

For example, if you are a physician and are passionate about your work, you are likely to know a lot about your specialty, and also about the drugs that are prescribed for illnesses within your specialty, about instruments and technology used to treat patients and, of course, about the medical-reimbursement system—health and hospital insurance. If you chose to focus on any one of these, you can quickly build up a store of knowledge that will rival any analyst, and put you in a position to profit from changes within that market.

You say that you like cars? More than a decade ago, Maryann Keller, a well-known auto-industry analyst, noted that it was possible to make good money investing in the automobile industry, even though it has one of the lowest industry P/E multiples of any industrial group. Keller's theory: By closely tracking the industry's goings-on, you would know when to buy and when to sell. And that—and not the size of the P/E—is one of the real keys to beating Wall Street.

Being involved with what you like led me to marketplace checks. I've always been interested in trends and in the latest new concept or product. So while I was still teaching, I began to do some work for a money manager named Claude Rosenberg, of Rosenberg Capital Management in San Francisco. Claude and his staff went out into the market and asked people what products they were buying, and then used that information to make decisions on stocks. That's marketplace checking at its simplest, and it provided higher returns for Claude's portfolio. Claude did much the same thing I am doing now, but in a more limited fashion. He followed fewer companies, and he took in information from fewer sources. Claude hired me to set up a division called Grassroots Research which went into the marketplace and asked competitors, suppliers, and customers their opinions of a company's products. Claude's and my work on getting unbiased marketplace checks helped RCM outperform their peers for ten years.

While I was happy working for Claude and probably would have stayed at RCM if he had stayed involved in the process, it occurred to me that there were even more sophisticated ways to apply the system of marketplace checks for all kinds of institutional investors. So, in 1994, I left Rosenberg Capital Management and formed OTR. Marketplace checking, going out into the market and finding out what people are buying—or not buying— and then supplying that information to institutional investors is all we do.

Every week, my staff of 150 people, who are located in cities all around the world, make hundreds of phone calls to people who work in 75 different industries, and ask them questions about what they are buying and what's selling. If we call computer retailers, we ask them what brands of computers people are buying.

Often, when a new product or service comes along, we can't go to a retailer. Increasingly, many products are sold directly. So, for example, when a phone company introduces a new technology like Digital Subscriber Loop (DSL) to provide its customers with much faster access to the Web, we call up the customers and ask them if they have subscribed to the service, whether they are using it, and how they like it. Most important, we ask them if they are recommending it to their customers and business contacts.

We report what we find, in a series of bulletins and briefs, to our subscriber base of institutional money managers and other Wall Street clients. They take that information and factor it into their own models, and then they decide whether it is time to buy or sell a stock. Marketplace checking is marketplace intelligence and, like all raw intelligence, it has to be sifted through and applied rigorously. When companies add our information to the information they have on hand, a clearer picture of what is going on in the economy and within companies begins to emerge.

Incidentally, marketplace checking is not limited just to learning about companies. Moses sending Joshua into Canaan to do marketplace checks is classic intelligence collection. In fact, the CIA used to be one of the largest marketplace checkers. Their reporters were called agents, and they sent back reams of information. But in the 1970s, the CIA began to abandon its spy networks in favor of technology—spy satellites and listening systems—the same way that Wall Street began to abandon rigorous research in favor of number crunching and high-speed computers.

And that's when the CIA's intelligence gathering began to degrade. What was once one of the best sources of hard information has turned into a bunch of technologically bound decision makers who are constantly in the dark.

The ultimate embarrassment probably came in the midst of NATO's bombing of Belgrade during the recent Balkan conflicts. NATO warplanes bombed the Chinese embassy because the CIA had old information on the embassy's location and had not updated its information by talking to people in Belgrade.

5

How You Can Become
a Marketplace Checker

I've spent some time talking about how I became a marketplace checker and what it has done for me. I'd like to spend just a little time telling you why *you* should become a marketplace checker and why it will benefit *you*.

Americans live in a marketplace society, and they lead transactional lives. Virtually everything we do, everything we are, everything we hold dear, comes about because of a transaction.

In the transactional world, your own individual transactions mean almost nothing. It is only when they are added up that patterns begin to emerge. Here's an example: You are driving down the road, getting increasingly hungry. You come to one of those crossroads that are increasingly common in American towns. There is a McDonald's on one side, a Burger King across the street, a KFC on the next corner, and perhaps a Wendy's or a Taco Bell on the fourth corner. Where you eat is entirely up to you and your individual tastes. But when you drive into or past the McDonald's, and you notice the sign under the golden arches that says "billions and billions sold," they are, if anything, undercounting. Americans today eat approximately one-third of their meals out. That's an average of one meal per day for 280 million people, 365 days a year. That comes to a staggering 102.2 billion meals eaten out every year. Almost one-third of those are eaten in fast-food restaurants. If the average fast-food check is $5, then one single share point in the fast-food wars is worth $1.32 billion, so where you and a lot of people decide to not eat becomes extremely important. Remember: You alone are unimportant. You and everybody else *together* are terribly important when it comes to the market and looking for investment opportunities.

Another example: Smoking has been on the decline in the United States for more than twenty years. But 32 million people still smoke at least one pack of cigarettes a day, which is nearly 11.7 billion packs of cigarettes a year. You might not think much of Philip Morris or RJR, but those 11.7 billion packs represent a huge amount of revenue. Again, with that many packs of cigarettes sold, it isn't how much you smoke, or what you smoke that is important. It is that 32 million people are smoking that counts.

The same concept holds for cars, or toothpaste, or soup, or any item where millions of people are making individual consumption decisions daily. Each transaction counts for almost nothing, much like a grain of sand. Together they are an endless beach. If you take all of the brands of any given product, and begin to count up how much of each people are buying, you begin to understand how one company is doing vis-à-vis another—and that's where you have the beginnings of an investment insight that can make you money.

So how do you count all of those grains of sand? Checking the pulse of the marketplace is simple. It merely requires that you go out and talk to people—lots of people. It also requires an inquisitive mind, some common sense, and a methodology for making sense of what you've heard. We'll provide lots of examples in this chapter, and show you how marketplace checks can be used to check up on existing companies, for trend spotting, for locating new business opportunities, for analyzing the fiscal health of your community, and for establishing a comparative base for your research. Often, what you observe will be at odds with what is going on in other parts of the country, so you have to be able to acquire the same kinds of information that you are looking for from other people in other places. That's where the power of the Internet emerges. We'll show you how to develop your own Internet marketplace-check information pool.

Let's start with the obvious: people. Do you already belong to an investment club? If so, you have a group of people whom you know, who are like-minded, who are reasonably intelligent, and who want to make money from investing. If you are going to use marketplace checking to help guide your investment decisions, all of you should read this chapter and discuss it. If you are not a member of an investment club, you can use the Internet, or what MCI used to call your "friends and family circle." Almost everybody networks to some extent; so if you can learn to use your own network of friends, relatives, coworkers and other associates with whom you come into regular contact, you can build up a body of people who will help you in the marketplace-check process.

First, you ought to agree which stocks you are going to follow. With a little bit of work, you can "reach out" to companies. Find someone who knows someone who works at one of the companies you want to track, and then pull that person into your circle. Let's say that your goal is to find an employee at high-flying telecommunications-equipment maker Qualcomm, or equally high-flying Broadvision, a company that provides Web-based customer-service tools. Both companies are headquartered in California, but let's say you live in rural Maine, which is about as far away physically as you can get from either company and still be in the continental United States. You have many choices on how to begin getting closer.

You can start with *Hoover's Handbook of American Business,* a large, multivolume index of companies we mentioned earlier. Hoover's will tell you about most large companies, and about their customers and their competition. Or you can go to a company's Web site. Many companies post extensive financial information on their sites, as well as detailed descriptions of their products and, often, lists of their largest customers. Now you have a much larger list of companies to work from. For example, Broadvision's site says that its customers include American Airlines, Circuit City, Credit Suisse, Fingerhut, Hartford Insurance, Home Depot, ING Bank, Macromedia, Merck, Nortel Networks, Hewlett-Packard, Intuit, Philips, Solectron, Sony, USAA, Warner Brothers, and Xerox, among established companies. So, if you don't know anybody who works at Broadvision, its customer list provides additional places to look for people who might know something about the company. Ask among your investment-club members, or your circle of friends and family if they know anyone at any of these firms, and if they don't, who they know who might. You have to be a little persistent in following up, but you will make a connection if you keep trying.

If nobody knows anybody at any of these companies, what about the companies or customers of these companies? Merck, for example, is a drug company. It sells to doctors and hospitals and pharmacies. Ask your doctor or pharmacist if a Merck drug representative makes sales calls, and if you could talk to the rep. When you talk to the rep, ask if he or she knows anyone at the company who works in data processing. Get a name, and ask to use the rep's name when you make the call.

You then pick up the phone and say, "Hi. My name is John Smith. I was talking to the Merck rep in my area, Miss Jones, and she gave me your name and number. I'm doing some research on Broadvision, and I understand that Merck is a customer of Broadvision. I don't want you to tell me anything that is a violation of company policy, but I'd like to ask you a couple of questions about Broadvision. It will take only a minute or two of your time."

Even if the person you are talking with has no direct connection with managing Merck's relationship with Broadvision, if this person is in data processing, he or she is likely to know the person who *does* work with Broadvision. Once you have that name, you can attempt to get that person to tell you something about what's going on at Broadvision—at least, from Merck's perspective.

Once that employee agrees to talk to you, you have to make your time count. There are several pieces of information you want to know. The most important question: "Is Merck a satisfied Broadvision customer?" If so, is Merck going to buy more services from Broadvision in the future and, if so, is it the near future or further out?

Next, you want to know if that Merck employee is a member of a Broadvision user group. Are there any other Broadvision customers he or she knows who might talk to you? Getting additional people to talk with lessens the chance that you will be listening to a skewed view of Merck's relationship with Broadvision. You build a network partly by enlisting the help of the people you've already talked with. Basically, you want to talk to enough people, and ask each of them essentially the same questions, so that you end up with enough information, and that it is of sufficient quality to allow you to make a decision about the stock.

What you learn from those questions is the following: If a company is satisfied and thinks that its relationships represent fair value, they are likely to remain customers. That translates into some level of future sales, which is what you want to know if you are going to attempt to forecast Broadvision's future earnings potential. The second question tells you how soon they

67

are going to make another purchase. If they are going to order tomorrow, that's more important to the near-term share price than if they are going to order next year. Since different companies are in different phases of their ordering and use cycles, ideally what you'd like to see is a mix of near-term and long-term orders. That would mean that Broadvision's revenues are likely to continue to grow at a decent rate, since presumably they would be adding new customers at the same time that they are filling orders from existing customers.

Once you have created enough links to cover the companies in which you are interested, you can begin to apply a checking process against those companies through your group. For example, let's say that one of the companies you decided to follow is Wal-Mart. Wal-Mart is huge, it has a presence in many towns, and it has maintained strong growth for several decades, so that it is now the largest retailer in the world. Since most Wal-Marts are pretty much alike, and carry mostly the same products, it's pretty easy to have your circle of friends and family fan out across the country every couple of days to see what is selling, and what is not selling at their local Wal-Mart. Pick any checkout aisle and just make some mental notes of what people are buying. Is it seasonal merchandise, like Christmas wrapping paper or Valentine's Day goods, or is it necessities, like paper goods? Are people buying a lot of toys, or are they spending more money on food?

When you've finished looking at what people are buying, take a walk into Wal-Mart's parking lot. Are the cars old or new? Are they low-end compacts or higher end full-size or luxury cars. Were the people in the store young or old, or a mixture? Each group has its own buying habits. Make sure you schedule your visits at the same time and day. Noticing that the parking lot at the Home Depot is full one Sunday, and almost empty the next is not very useful if your second observation was taken on the day of the Super Bowl.

Next, try to get a mental fix on the profit margin on the items being purchased. If you see people buying a lot of toys, CDs, cameras, jewelry, and junk food (soda, pretzels and chips)—those are pretty high-margin items (Wal-Mart makes more on each dollar of sales). If you see people buying lots of food staples—canned goods, pasta, meats—and household detergent, those are low-margin items.

Look for items that are out of stock as that indicates a hot seller. Note which brands people are buying, because those choices show the ascendancy of one consumer-products company over another (e.g., Procter & Gamble vs. Colgate or Arm & Hammer).

If you think that tackling a company as large as Wal-Mart is beyond your abilities, consider this: If you had been tracking Wal-Mart by observing traffic in the parking lots, you would have noticed over the summer of 2000 that there were fewer cars in Wal-Mart's lots, which would have got you asking questions. You would have turned up what the company admitted in late September: Wal-Mart notified analysts that it would probably not meet analyst expectations on sales, because high gas prices and the prospects of high home-heating-oil prices for the winter were keeping people out of Wal-Mart's stores (which is why there were fewer cars in the parking lots). On that news, Wal-Mart's shares fell nearly 2 percent.

As you can see, marketplace checking is literally that: watching and observing what is going on in the world around you and turning those observations into detailed data, from which you can begin to draw inferences about the performance of specific companies. That process is called "collection and analysis." Collection and analysis is what intelligence agencies do. It is what reporters on newspapers do, and it is what good Wall Street analysts used to do.

As I said at the beginning of this chapter, marketplace checking has many applications. The most obvious one is to check up on the performance of existing companies. In any given field, there are probably dozens of companies that compete, and the larger the company, generally, the greater the number of companies that compete with it. This is counterintuitive. All your life, you've been told that big companies squash out competition, but the reality is that the larger a company is, the more product lines it is likely to have, and each one of those product lines has its own set of competitors. So a company like Sara Lee, which is in more than a dozen different lines of business, ranging from panty hose (L'eggs) to hot dogs (Ball Park Franks), has literally hundreds of competitors.

That makes it difficult to check the overall health of Sara Lee because it is difficult to know which product lines contribute the most to the company's profitability and which contribute the least. You can get that information by reading a lot of analysts' reports, but that isn't a marketplace-checking system. So how do you make your knowledge work for you? You could focus on Sara Lee's competitors, to see if you can find a smaller company that has certain characteristics. It needs to be small to medium in size—less than $1 billion in sales—and needs to have a limited product line. Finally, it needs to be public, so you can follow it easily.

These "mid-cap" companies, so named because their market capitalization—the total value of all their stock (number of outstanding shares multiplied by stock price)—is between about $500 million and $2 billion, are where it is possible to do some real marketplace checking. They are highly focused, usually having a single major product and some line extensions—other products that are similar to the main product but differentiated by price and features—and they are more in control of their own destiny than big companies are. A number of large institutions, such as Friess Associates in Delaware, make a specialty out of following mid-cap companies, and do very well at it. While they have been generally ignored by investors, who are looking for

70

huge returns from high-technology firms, or the stability of blue chip Dow 30 investments and well-known brand names, mid-caps are often where the action is.

Indeed, while everyone thinks that high growth is the way to make money, the real key to Wall Street profitability is mergers and acquisitions—M&A activity. Almost half the value of the overall stock market's rise over the past decade has come from increases in value from M&A activity, with very large companies swallowing up the shares of mid-cap companies, often at a hefty stock premium. The M&A wave never goes away. It just moves from industry to industry, as industrial groups go through successive waves of consolidation to create the efficiencies that lead to the profits that investors have come to expect. Find the industries most in need of consolidation and the companies that are most likely to be gobbled up, and you've found one of the keys to real investor success.

Mid-caps and smaller companies are also the area where you can use marketplace checking as a trend-spotting tool. Large companies, with few exceptions, such as Sony in consumer electronics, are generally not very innovative. They use their large distribution systems, their access to the widest variety of market channels, and their ability to buy raw materials more cheaply than their smaller competitors, to create efficiencies in the marketplace, allowing them to enter a developing market later and still win a large share. But when a large company cannot find an efficient way to enter a market on its own, it is likely to buy a smaller company.

There are other ways you can use marketplace checks to improve your investment returns. As a research system, the value of marketplace checks goes beyond stocks, into other investment areas:

1. Checking up on the economic health of your community. Very soon after I started writing this book, an article appeared on the front page of *The New York Times* that talked about how the Lehigh Valley, in Pennsylvania, where I went to school, was stealing jobs from neighboring New Jersey. The article went on to talk about how the valley, with its lower wages, open spaces, and a new Lucent Technologies plant, was becoming attractive to high-tech industries. And because it was on the Pennsylvania–New Jersey border, it was close to markets in Philadelphia and New York City. This article is a small piece of marketplace intelligence. If you own the bonds of the Lehigh Valley Industrial Authority, for example, a piece of news like that probably means that your bonds are suddenly worth a bit more. Bonds work just like stocks: When there is good news, the demand for bonds goes up, and investors will pay more in order to own a given bond. When there is bad news, those same investors want to sell those bonds, and their price drops.

This simple observation gives you the basis for setting up a system to do marketplace checks on your community. Go to one of the bond-rating agencies—Standard & Poor's, Moody's, or Duff & Phelps, and find out how the local bonds in your area are rated. Common types of bonds include municipal bonds, water-authority bonds, industrial bonds, airport-authority bonds, school-construction bonds, and other special-purpose financing, like the bonds for an athletic stadium. When you get the bond report, take a look at the assumptions behind the ratings, and if they aren't there, call the analyst whose name is on the report. The analyst can send you a report, which describes the local situation at the time the original rating was issued, as well as some of the financial assumptions on how the issuing authority was going to earn enough money to pay back the bonds.

Let's take a 30-year airport-authority bond for $10 million, paying 7 percent interest, issued in 1990. At the time, the Anywhere International Airport was handling 30 flights and 3,000 passengers per day. With an airport tax of $3 per head to amortize the bonds, plus $1 per day for each car parked in the airport's lots, plus a fee of $5,000 per year per car-rental company, plus a landing fee of $200 per plane, the airport would be earning about $5.8 million per year. To repay the bond, the airport authority has to make payments to bondholders of $333,333.33 per year in principal, plus $700,000 a year in interest, or $1.33 million together. If the airport is run properly, it has to operate on a budget of less than $4.5 million per year, and probably less than that, in order for the airport authority to accumulate some money for emergencies in a rainy-day fund.

But wait! It is now the year 2001. Every time you go to the airport to take a flight somewhere, the parking lot is full, and you have to park out in the boonies, in the long-term parking lot. You look at your ticket, and the airport departure tax is now $7.50, so you begin to scratch your head and do some numbers in your head. You look at the flight board and ask one of the ticket agents if the airport has gotten busier, and she groans and tells you that the airport is now running nearly 100 flights a day, and that a new airline is about to come into the airport with yet more flights.

You have the rating history, and you notice that there is absolutely no surge of demand for the bonds. What gives? Probably nothing. The rating authority wrote their original report when they priced the bonds, sold them to their accounts, and then forgot about them. You do some judicious checking, calling around to the chamber of commerce and the airport authority, and getting some publicly accessible records, which shows that the authority is taking in about $12 million a year, and is spending only about $7 million. This is an airport with a serious cash surplus, more than enough to retire the bonds.

What do you do? Because you've done your marketplace checking, and asked a lot of questions, you buy a bunch of the bonds, and then you call the local newspaper, the *Anywhere Gazette*. You tell the business editor that the airport has a major surplus, and that they really ought to retire the bonds early if they want to exercise good fiscal management. The paper sends a reporter to do the same marketplace checking that you've already done. Pretty soon, the story comes out, and the airport authority decides to retire the bonds early, paying a premium in cash to bondholders to compensate them for lost interest. You sell your newly purchased bonds at a nice profit and whistle the check into the bank.

Precisely because most municipal and authority bonds don't have a highly liquid market, enormous information disparities can and do crop up all the time, giving investors the opportunity to buy and sell bonds at a far larger profit than they might otherwise enjoy from simply buying and holding.

Checking up on the health of your community and its institutions is as simple as subscribing to the local newspaper and reading it religiously. If the local paper is any good, you will find news about companies that are hiring, companies that are moving into your area, and companies that are moving out. You will find out about new real-estate subdivisions, and how well the local authorities are spending your tax money. All of this is grist for your marketplace-checking mill. Because this is your local community, getting information is easy. Unless you live in a really large city, public officials are probably pretty accessible. Most communities hold open town- or city-council meetings, which very few people ever bother to attend. Aside from the fact that nothing much appears to happen, attending meetings is the best way to find out who you should be asking to get more information. For example, if there is a meeting about a new sewer system that is going to require a new bond issue, and one councilperson objects seriously, call that person in the morning, and ask them what the economic basis of the objection is. Are there studies which suggest that there won't be enough growth to support the new bond? Are there studies which suggest that the system itself is too expensive for what it delivers, or that it will require a large tax hike to pay for it? If you understand the basis of the objection, you can begin to understand whether or not the bond is going to be fairly priced.

Once you've called the opposition, call a couple of the sewer's supporters. Ask them the same questions and attempt to find out who is going to benefit from the sewer's construction. Often it will be a developer who is a large contributor to the party in power. If so, find out by asking questions how much the new subdivision is expected to add to the tax rolls, and how much of that money is going to go toward bond amortization. Even if you decide not to buy the bond, you're going to be much better informed about your city's local politics, and be in a position to decide which side you're going to support. And if you smell something fishy, you have enough ammunition to take your case to the newspaper.

2. Finding a new business opportunity. If you never leave your hometown, you aren't likely to see what people in other places are doing. But if you have friends in other towns and cities, and you are asking them about retailing trends, you might just be the first to spot the next Home Depot or the next Sports Authority. All large chain stores start somewhere—Home Depot began in Atlanta, Wal-Mart in rural Arkansas—and if you or one of your contacts see a new store, you can put it on a watch list and monitor it to see if it expands into other areas.

A good example of a store on the move is Trader Joe's, a small independent grocery chain that is expanding rapidly. Its stores up and down California are always on the hunt for interesting new foods and toiletries. Trader Joe's is a great place to check out not only new things to buy, but by watching what people buy, you can begin to discern trends. For example, there's been a wine boom in San Francisco for twenty years, but cheese has been pretty stable. I began to notice that Trader Joe's selection of cheeses was starting to grow, and that there were more and more people in the cheese section, buying more and more exotic cheeses. I don't know much about cheese, but I could tell that a cheese boom was in the making. Sure enough, the Safeway near me moved its cheese counter to the front of the store, and a specialty cheese shop opened up a couple of blocks from my house. Now, this is San Francisco, which is a little bit ahead in all sorts of cultural trends, but it is not as far ahead as you might think. The wine boom started here, but now Americans drink a lot of wine. So if there's a cheese boom in San Francisco, you can assume that Americans are soon going to be eating a lot of cheeses that are more exotic than mere cheddar and Cheez Whiz.

You say you don't go to San Francisco much? How about a trip through your town or the next town. Make some notes about what kinds of stores there are. See if there are any different kinds of businesses. If there are, ask yourself why, and then begin asking other people. If certain stores are missing, ask yourself why, and then ask other people. For example, back in the Lehigh Valley (that place again), there are no Starbucks, except an outpost in a Barnes & Noble just north of Allentown. However, there is a lot of gourmet coffee being sold in small drive-up outlets with names like Mocha Mike's and Latte Lorrie's. This could mean one of two things: either there is an opportunity for Starbucks to expand, or there isn't. Call Starbucks and ask them about their plans for the Lehigh Valley (or your own area, since that's where you'll be looking). Ask Mike and Lorrie why their coffee sells well, and why they think there is no Starbucks. Ask some of the people who drive up to these outlets. They are the potential customer base, the people who are already buying gourmet coffee from someone. By doing the legwork, you can find out what's going on. From that, you can determine whether there is a good business opportunity for you in going into the gourmet-coffee business, or if there is something peculiar about the Lehigh Valley that makes it off-limits to Starbucks, and therefore limits its expansion potential, and therefore, its future earnings potential.

Just because you see something in your travels that appeals to you, that doesn't mean that it will come to your hometown automatically. But if you see a store you've never seen before, and it is suddenly opening outlets all over the place, start looking for that store as an investment opportunity. Go to the Web and find out more. Is the company public? If so, rapid expansion can often mean that the company has developed a profitable formula for merchandising, or has found a niche to exploit. Look at the stock price. If it isn't moving, start asking questions. You may have found a winner. If the company is not public, find out who owns it and what their plans might be. In any event, learn to keep track of the store as a potential investment.

Often, when you see a retailer in a particular town, you are seeing a reflection of the demographics of that place. And demographics, the study of the characteristics of large clusters of people—their ages, incomes, education levels, ethnicity, and other characteristics—helps to determine much of what people buy. For example, if you see that a relatively small town has two or three medical-supply stores that sell convalescent equipment, it's a sure bet that the town has an aging population. If you see that the town has a number of stores selling Pokemon cards, it's an equally sure bet that the town has a lot of little boys between the ages of seven and ten. You can use demographic trends in either a forward or backward direction to spot investment opportunities, and when you combine it with marketplace checking, you will very often come up with a good investment opportunity before anyone else does.

What do we mean by "backward" and "forward"? You can work backward from an existing business to identify a demographic group, and then figure out what else that group might want to buy. For example, take the medical-equipment stores as an indicator of an aging population. If you do a little checking with your local county planning board, they will tell you how many seniors there are in the town and in surrounding communities. They will probably even have some projections on the future growth of the senior population. By asking a couple of additional questions, you can learn the characteristics of those seniors—their ages, their average state of health, their income ranges, and their medical needs. You might find that there are enough seniors so that you can start thinking about what other sorts of businesses would appeal to them—for example, a store that sells senior-friendly appliances with over-sized handles and other ergonomically designed tools, or a store that sells hobby gear.

If the seniors are generally young and vigorous, you might want to think about a store that sells golf and other athletic equipment, like bikes and good walking shoes. You don't want to use that information to start a business—although you could—but rather, to find out what a particular group is buying and what they are likely to buy next. Once you know what they are purchasing, and who makes it, you can judge how companies are doing in the marketplace. That can be translated into investment decisions.

Or you can work forward from a given demographic group. Let's stick with senior citizens. If there are a lot of seniors in your town, start talking to them, asking them questions about what they are buying and consuming, and what sorts of things they'd like to spend their money on if it was available in town. By asking questions, you can find opportunities, even when none seemingly exist. And by asking them in a marketplace-checking framework, you will be cutting down on the random element, so that your questions will lead to answers with investment potential.

3. Trend spotting. If marketplace checks are good for finding new opportunities, they are great for spotting trends. A trend is something innovative done by a person or a group that is likely to be done by larger groups of people once the idea behind the trend is widely accepted. In the United States, which is an extremely fluid society, connected by mass-media outlets such as television and the movies, new trends form and sweep across the country all the time. If you can learn to spot trends, you can make money from them.

Of course, you must learn the difference between a trend and a fad. Both will make money for someone, but a fad will usually make money for only a few individuals. Pet rocks were a fad that made money only for the company that dreamed them up, and the people who sold them. When other companies tried to get into the pet-rock business, the fad collapsed, and nobody made any more money. But a trend is different. Trends beget entire industries, and create employment, infrastructure, and major opportunities for large numbers of people.

In the 1970s, Xerox had already invented the office computer as we know it today. It had a mouse, a graphic user interface, pull-down menus, and a host of other features we take for granted in computers. The Xerox Star, as the computer was called, also cost a fortune—more than $10,000 per installation, at a time when the average family income was only about $20,000 a year. The machine's memory was tiny, and there were few programs to power it.

While the Xerox Star was an important development, desktop computing began essentially as a fad. But there were people who saw the potential of desktop computing, among them Bill Gates and Steve Jobs. Jobs and his partner, Steve Wozniak, visited Xerox's Palo Alto Research Center (PARC) and came away with the idea of building an affordable "personal" computer that employed much of the technology that already existed in the Xerox Star. Bill Gates, then a young student at Harvard, properly foresaw that it was less the hardware—and more the operating system that allowed all of the parts of the computer to work together—that was the key to personal-computer success, so he purchased an existing operating system, Q-DOS (for

Quick and Dirty Operating System) and built a giant company around it called Microsoft.

The combination of those two elements, low-cost personal computers, and a reliable operating system, created the personal-computer industry which, in turn, has spawned a dozen other industries, ranging from hardware, chip manufacturing and software, to the Internet and wireless telecommunications—industries that employ millions of people, as well as generating billions of dollars of purchases and wealth.

Technology is only one kind of trend. Other forms of trends are social, legal, and business trends. All of them become visible through a marketplace-check approach to asking questions. Let's take a simple example. You go to your doctor for a sore knee, and he diagnoses a touch of arthritis. He writes you a prescription for a new drug called Vioxx, instead of the usual ibuprofen- or naproxen-based drug he normally gives you. This starts you asking him questions. Is this a better form of therapy?

Is he writing a lot of prescriptions for the new drug? Does he know of other doctors who are prescribing it? You can then ask your pharmacist the same questions and call a few other doctors and pharmacies. Pretty soon you have a good local base of information.

Now you get on the telephone or the Internet, and you begin asking other people if they have noticed the same behavior. If you have built up a circle of friends, this won't be too difficult to do. They will begin asking their own doctors and pharmacists if there has been a shift in arthritis prescriptions. If so, you have a trend, albeit a minor one. It's probably sufficient to make an investment decision on, once you've done a little more checking.

But wait—there's more! If you really want to spot a trend, you have to ask the more important questions about Vioxx and other drugs like it, such as *why* did so many doctors begin to change the medication they were writing. Your doctor will tell you that the new drug not only takes the pain of arthritis away, but also the inflammation, allowing people who previously had been incapacitated to the point of immobility suddenly to begin walking again.

"Why" questions begin to lead you to discover trends. If a new drug has a major impact on the way people live their lives, a whole new set of winners and losers is created. For example, if many people who previously were not ambulatory can suddenly walk again and use their hands, it means that they can begin to lead productive lives. Perhaps that means nothing more than an increase in the amount of money spent on gardening equipment and plants. But combined with relaxed Social Security rules about how much money seniors can make, perhaps it means a large surge of senior citizens into the workforce.

If you want to use marketplace checks to spot trends, you must be able to both see the larger picture and interpret it properly. Very few people are good at either spotting trends, or of interpreting them well because it is very difficult to figure out how one thing can lead to another. But it is not as difficult as you might think, especially if you have a reasonably wide circle of people to talk with on an ongoing basis. If you see something that you think might be the start of a trend, begin to track it on a regular basis.

Let's stick with our Vioxx example. Write down everything you can think of that might result from people being more active, and what might result from those things. For instance, if people can suddenly walk comfortably, they might go to places where a lot of walking is required. That might be the local mall, but it might also be Disney World. If it's Disney World, then people are going to do more driving or flying and, in any event, they will spend more money on meals out, and at hotels. At this point, you're probably going to say to yourself, "How can there be such a ripple effect from a change in drug prescriptions?" Here's the answer: Ours is a gigantic economy, so even small changes generate very large dollars. For each 1 percent of the U.S. population that changes its habits in some way, the result is billions of dollars in sales shifted from one place to another.

For example, approximately twenty states currently have electricity-choice programs. During the 1990s, many states decided that deregulating the way companies supplied electricity would generate savings for consumers. In those states that have deregulated, the average consumer saves about 15 percent of his or her electric bill. That is actually not a large savings, since most people don't pay a lot for electricity, anyway. But the total electricity-generating business in the United States is $250 billion, so each 1 percent shift from one supplier to another is worth $2.5 billion. Now, in California and Pennsylvania, customers can buy electricity from environmentally friendly suppliers, who use wind power and hydropower, or methane from landfills, or clean-burning natural gas. Overall, only 2 percent of all customers who have been allowed to switch have actually done so, but in California, 95 percent of those switching have chosen environmental alternatives and, in Pennsylvania, 20 percent of switchers have gone the "green" route.

This has meant at least a $6 billion windfall for the companies that supply clean energy, and generally, as California goes, so goes the rest of the country. So this tiny little blip could become a major trend, with huge implications not only for the power industry and "green" suppliers, but also for their nongreen fuel-supplying competitors like coal, oil, and natural gas. (In June 2000, Amoco made a $100 million investment in Green Mountain Energy, the major supplier of clean alternative-energy sources, confirming that a trend was in the making.)

How do you apply a marketplace-check strategy to this situation? You ask your neighbors what they plan to do. If only 2 percent of people have switched so far, that leaves 98 percent of people who have not switched electricity suppliers. Perhaps people don't really understand the advantages of making a change.

Perhaps they believe that someone will have to come to their house and disconnect their power and hook up someone else's line. Perhaps they are simply happy with their existing supplier, or believe that the trouble of filling out paperwork to make the switch is not worth the amount of money that will be saved.

But remember: each 1 percent of switchers is worth $2.5 billion to someone. To the extent that you can ascertain potential changes in consumer behavior by asking people about it, you can get a good sense of where the electricity-switching market is heading. If you have your group ask the same questions to a larger and wider audience, you will know with even more certainty whether the trend is 1 or 2 percent, or a potentially much larger shift. (Incidentally, you might also find yourself with a new business opportunity in helping people make the switch. If many people tell you that they would change, but that they can't be bothered with the paperwork, you can do the work for them at a fee, or launch a Web site that helps them make their decision. If you think that idea makes no sense, take a look at a Web site called Cellmania.com, which helps people choose the right cell phone. Such services do well because people really are lazy, or because doing such research is too time consuming given the relatively small amount of money involved.)

4. Looking at the comparative health of companies. Friends of mine who worked at *Forbes* magazine tell me there was a standing rule about asking questions before writing a story. The rule was, "Who wins? Who loses? Who is helped and who is hurt?"

The idea behind those four questions is simple: No company exists in a vacuum, and for every winner, there are bound to be a couple of losers. This is what is known as a "zero-sum game." That is, any given environment is essentially a closed loop, so that if you add something on one side of a closed system, you have to subtract an equal amount on the other side.

However, societies like ours are not really closed loops. People are born every day, so there is a slow, steady growth of new customers. And with steady inputs of technology, habits and buying patterns change slowly as well. Still, for the most part, the "zero-sum" analogy works reasonably well, and most companies operate within a limited, semiclosed universe, where each point of gain in their market share means at least a partial point loss for a competitor. This is where marketplace checks really excel. If you know the market shares of various competitors at some given point in time for any given category of product, you can begin to rapidly and accurately track who is hurt and who is helped just by asking people what they are purchasing.

The zero-sum game can even be seen in segments of the technology market. PDAs (personal digital assistants) first came out as advanced notebooks and calendars. They were thought of as high-tech address books. As Palm and Handspring continued to make improvements and add additional functions, the PDA began to compete with the PC (especially the laptop version) as the first-line technological device of the Twenty-first-century man (and woman and child). As the emphasis went from computing to communications, PDAs and the hybrid HPCs (Handheld Personal Computers) have begun to compete with PC sales. In the next few years, the PDA could replace the PC as the primary technological tool.

There are a few other areas where marketplace checks come in handy for checking the comparative health of companies. Many companies have large international divisions and get a sizable amount of their sales and profits from abroad. Many Wall Street analysts, because they are geared to following American companies and sales, ignore the impact of international sales until quarterly earnings have come out, by which time it's too late, of course. The only time that Wall Street responds to changes abroad over the short term is when there are major currency or political crises overseas. If the British pound or the Euro were to suffer a steep decline in price, for example, Wall Street would downgrade many companies that have large-scale operations in Europe, on the theory that goods sold there would cost more when translated back into dollars, and there-fore would result in lower profits for American companies. But most of the time, the impact of overseas markets is not factored into Wall Street's equation.

That disregard provides a great opportunity for marketplace checkers, and it also provides you with an opportunity to get to know some new people. Since 1969, America has been flooded with new immigrants from all over the world, many who retain strong ties with their families and friends back home. Include some of those immigrants in your circles.

The process is actually pretty simple. Once you decide to follow a particular company and get its annual report, you can look in the financial sections and determine how much of the company's sales come from abroad. These numbers are also given when *Forbes* and *Fortune* publish their 500 issues every spring. Once you have a copy of one of those magazines, call the company's investor-relations office to find out which of four or five countries account for the majority of sales and profits. Once you discover them, finding nationals of those countries in the United States, which is a nation of immi-grants, is also not difficult. It means asking existing members of your circle if they know people from these countries, and if they could ask those people, when they call home, to ask some marketplace-check-oriented questions about the companies you want to follow.

So, for example, if you are following J&J, and you read in the annual report that sales in Eastern Europe, especially the Czech Republic, are up 50 percent in the past year, and that such sales now account for 10 percent of J&J's overseas revenues and 14 percent of its profits, it doesn't take many calls to find someone who knows a recent Czech immigrant. Call that person and ask for a hand in getting some information on markets in the Czech Republic, and then explain what you want to know.

This might sound like a completely hit-or-miss approach to finding information, but it isn't. Just as people are connected to each other here, people in other countries are connected to each other through networks of family, friends, and education. The difference is that in the United States, people are spread out, while in a small nation like the Czech Republic, people are highly concentrated. That makes reaching the right people much easier than here.

Moreover, once you find key people, they will probably know several other well-connected people who can give you information on other companies that do business in the Czech Republic. Years ago, Walt Rostow, who was an adviser to President Lyndon Johnson, developed what he called "the theory of continually circulating elites": Power in most countries is concentrated in the hands of only a few groups, who move in and out of positions of power in business, education, and government. Once you can tap into one of the groups, you can gain information on literally everything that is going on in a country. In the case of a Czech immigrant to the United States, you will likely be talking to someone who is at least a peripheral member of one of those elite groups. If you cultivate that person by offering to pay something toward their monthly international phone bills, you will have made a staunch ally. The more material the information is to you, the more valuable it is.

6

FIND THE EXPERTS

The Ten Rules for Establishing a Marketplace-Checking System

In this chapter, we'll show you how to set up a research group among your investment club or your friends in more detail. Not everybody you meet is going to be good at marketplace checking. It is a learnable skill, but it requires levels of curiosity and persistence that many people don't have, and it requires time. I have a staff of people who do marketplace checks for a living, but you are going to have to do them while you are also running your life. That means you are going to have to fit your phone calls into your otherwise-busy day. It can be done, if you have a solid group of people, and if you limit the number of companies you are going to track.

Here are the Ten Rules of Marketplace Relations, which you need to live by to form your research team, and to reward the people who help you out. If you are working by yourself, you will not be able to follow all of the rules to the same degree as a group of people can. It will be too time consuming and too impractical. But you should know what the rules are, and attempt to follow them as best you can.

1. Some people are clearly better at research than others. At Off The Record Research, we rely upon a network of reporters around the world to get us the information we need. Many of these people have journalism backgrounds, which means that they have been trained to observe, to ask questions, and to report in a structured way. This process is often called "CAD," for Collection, Analysis, and Dissemination, and it is a process that is used by journalists, intelligence agents, police and Wall Street security analysts alike all over the world.

Collection is the process of gathering information. Some people are naturally good observers. They have a combination of curiosity about the world around them, coupled with the ability to dig for information by asking questions. Most people lack either one trait or the other. They might be curious, but they either don't want to ask questions, fearing they'll rile people around them, or they don't know how. They don't know when they've seen something that's important. They'll look at a situation, something will nag at them, and then they will be distracted by the next situation. Obviously, they are not likely to make good members of your marketplace check team.

Analysis is what you do with the information once you get it. Are the people who are helping you able to generate insights based upon what they've observed, or out of the questions they've asked? Are they able to take the information and put it into a form that you will find useful? If not, don't worry, because Chapter 9 will teach you some simple methods for making sense out of the information you've collected, so that if the analytical skills of your people aren't very high, it won't matter too much.

Dissemination is just a fancy word for where the report goes. In a newspaper, the reporter's collection and analysis—his story—is disseminated to the widest possible audience via the newspaper. Government intelligence officers, do their collection without anyone noticing (we hope), and write a report that is going to be seen by only a very few eyes (we hope). In between, there is a whole range of information collected, analyzed, and disseminated to relatively small audiences.

Wall Street research falls into this category. Companies like Strong, Merrill Lynch, and Fidelity pay companies like ours lots of money for information that will not be seen all over the place. They take that information and incorporate it into their own models and, in turn, sell it to their customers at equally high prices.

This limited-dissemination model is the way that you will operate. When you are setting up your marketplace-check system, you want the people who help you to clearly understand, from the beginning, that the information that you all agree to share is not to be shared with the outside world. You don't want someone in your investment group telling his cousin about a hot investment tip because that increases the likelihood that the information you've worked so hard to dig up will be disseminated widely before you have the best chance to make your investment. If the members of your group don't gain the benefit of all of your collective work, then what is the point of doing the work in the first place? I am not advocating that you become secretive or paranoid about what you are doing, but rather, that you understand that the work of marketplace checking has value, and that you and your collective group ought to be the first people to profit.

Now, back to the people themselves. Who makes the best marketplace checkers for your team? Reporters, for one. Newspaper reporters have been trained to ask questions and, even when they are not especially curious, they are persistent, and will keep hunting around until they get enough details to write a story. (Or in the case of a marketplace check, they will have collected enough information to help you form a conclusion.) But most journalists are pretty busy working to make a living, and if there is no quick monetary payoff, your chances of getting a good business journalist into your group are pretty small.

Since it's hard to get reporters, find experts in the stocks you want to cover. If you are interested in medical stocks, find some doctors and pharmacists, especially a few who have some connections to the larger medical establishment. Surgeons are visited by pharmaceutical-company representatives and equipment reps far more than pediatricians are. Internists get a huge number of visits, as do physicians who specialize in the care of older people. If you are interested in high technology, pick an area, such as telecommunications, and then look for people with some expertise; people who work for companies like Lucent or Cisco or Nokia or Ericsson. If you want to follow packaged goods or food companies, look for people who spend a lot of time in supermarkets and drugstores, or who do wholesale purchasing for large retail companies. By choosing people who have some familiarity with the industries that you are covering, you can be assured that you will get better analysis. These experienced people know what is important in their industry and what is not.

What other traits do you want in your people? You want people who are conscientious about doing their work because time is crucial in marketplace checking. You are looking to discover insights about the companies that your group is following before Wall Street does, so it is important that information collection and analysis be done promptly. There is nothing worse than getting your information a day or two late, and finding that the marketplace has already discovered what your group thinks is original, and observing that the market has already reacted. This is especially true for positive information because the market is always looking for good stories. The stock markets tend to ignore bad news for a bit longer, before overreacting and then dumping a stock.

What if you don't have a group and are determined to do your marketplace checks by yourself? Then you have to narrow your focus even more. Concentrate on a single sector—for example, telecommunications—and find an expert whose opinion you can trust. You will have to subscribe to industry newsletters and trade magazines, and do a lot of reading, and then bounce your potential analytical insights off your expert for confirmation or modification. It's harder, but it's doable.

2. Recognize patterns. The ability to synthesize from experience is a second key to doing marketplace checks. Psychologists call this aptitude "pattern recognition," and this ability to see patterns rapidly is the hallmark of the good analyst. For example, from early 1999 through April 2000, Federal Reserve Chairman Alan Greenspan raised interest rates repeatedly, and there has been a recurring pattern in the stock market.

The first time that Greenspan raised rates, the market reacted after the fact by falling the next day, then surging ahead. The second time, the market reacted by falling on the announcement, and then surging ahead again. The third time, the market reacted a couple of days before what was an anticipated announcement, and then surged ahead again. The fourth time, the market reacted even earlier, and then surged ahead yet again.

By the fifth time, it was becoming clear that Greenspan's ability to make the market tumble was being constrained by the market's ability to anticipate the fact that he was going to raise rates. In fact, editorials began to appear which suggested that the Fed chairman's ability to control the market had disappeared, and that he was reacting in such a reflexive way that the pattern of his behavior had become too predictable.

That left Greenspan with two alternatives: either to raise rates sooner than expected to catch the market off guard, or to raise them more than anticipated, to show that he meant business. He chose the first course of action, and the stock markets finally got the message in April 2000, cooling off considerably. Wall Street is run by a lot of very smart people, and when they recognize a pattern, they eventually react the way they are supposed to.

When you see a pattern emerging, learn to act quickly. For example, if you see that a stock you are following rises and falls on a fairly regular basis, find out why. It may be that the company is responding to a very predictable business cycle. If so, learn to buy as the stock is beginning to rise, and sell just before the stock hits its peak. You can go into the same stock several times, and make money each time. (Sometimes the spreads are fairly narrow. R.R. Donnelley & Sons, a commercial printer, which supplies online courses for corporations, has been trading within a seven-point range for all of 2000. The stock went up to between $2,750 and $2,652, and then fell to between $19,504 and $2,246. Following a company's rise and fall can be very profitable.)

Aside from pattern recognition, smart people can also generally see things that don't fall into patterns, or anomalies. Many of the best marketplace insights come from being the first to notice something that is outside of the ordinary, and to be able to recognize that it might be a new pattern. Futurist Faith Popcorn (that's not her real name, it's a nom de marketing) has made quite a nice living for herself in recognizing these new patterns and selling her insights to companies. She was responsible for seeing that people in the early 1990s were going to be more interested in their homes than in outside socializing; she called this trend "cocooning," and she propelled companies like Home Depot and Lowe's, and all of the companies that made home-improvement products and furniture and home furnishings to new heights of profitability once everyone else realized that this trend was for real.

The recent book *Bobos in Paradise,* by David Brooks, does much the same thing. Bobos, or bourgeois bohemians, are the well-educated elite that have replaced the traditional WASP elite of the United States. Brooks's key insight rests on the fact that this elite has swelled from 2 million households with incomes above $100,000 to 9 million in only a decade. This group, which challenges authority and is self-actualizing, will set social trends—and buying trends—for at least a decade to come, Brooks argues. These people are more likely to buy from Pottery Barn and Restoration Hardware than in stores like Wal-Mart and Home Depot, driving their sales upward.

Our own insights are perhaps not as sexy, but they do pay off. In July 1998 we noticed that the strong economy was keeping construction spending high, and that the trend was likely to continue even in the face of rising interest rates. So we told our clients that Caterpillar would likely continue doing well. Caterpillar stock went from 47 to 65 within six months. Not only Caterpillar benefited from the strong economy. We also noticed that there was a shortage of big trucks. Strong economic growth, inventory buildups because of Y2K fears, and the diversion of shipments from rail to trucks because of poor service by railroads were leading to tight capacity in the trucking market. The beneficiary, we told our clients, was likely to be Landstar System Inc. Its stock rose 70 percent between August 1999 and the end of that year.

3. Buyers and sellers are key people. Within your marketplace-checking group, it really helps to have people who have direct experience with the products of the companies that you are following. If you are following drug and medical-equipment stocks, it really helps to have a couple of doctors who are prescribing, and who are being visited regularly, by drug reps. You will also help your team if you have a couple of pharmacists, or if you can find a pharmacist who runs the dispensary in a hospital, or who is in charge of ordering the hospital's supplies. These buyers and sellers have the greatest direct perspective on what is happening in the marketplace, so you want to get them onto your team. If they are not on your team, then you certainly want them for your panels.

Panels are groups of people that your team will interview on a regular basis. So, for example, when you are putting together your team, and you've gotten a couple of doctors and pharmacists, you want them, in turn, to interview many more doctors and pharmacists whom they know. The reason is that the larger the number of people who say something is true, the higher the probability that it is true. If one doctor tells you that he is writing a lot of prescriptions for Wellbutrin instead of Prozac, that might be a coincidence. But if fifty physicians around the country all tell you the same thing, then you know that Wellbutrin is supplanting Prozac, and that there is a shift in the relative fortunes of the companies that make each drug.

If pharmaceuticals don't interest you, but you think money can be made in fast food, the methodology I describe here is equally useful. You can make money from any stock or group of stocks, and fast food is no exception. But in order to do this right, you have to look at a larger group of companies than just McDonald's or Burger King. You have to look at the entire world of eating. You have to examine supermarket sales, sales at fast-food outlets, slightly more upmarket dinner restaurants like Red Lobster and Outback Steakhouse, and the local fancy restaurants. This is a massive undertaking, so you need a few boundaries to help you out.

The simplest way to find out how many people are using the local fast-food and other restaurant outlets in your town is to count cars in the parking lot. But that takes a lot of people, so you don't want to sit there counting every car in every lot. You want to find out which chains are doing special promotions, and then count the number of people who are responding to them, compared to the weeks when there is no promotion going on. For example, does "Lobster Fest" pull a lot of people into your local Red Lobster? What about McDonald's Monopoly game promotion, or Burger King's Pokémon promotion? You know that the parent companies are spending heavily on advertising to drive traffic, so if you don't see a big uptick in cars in the lot, or going past the drive-thru, it's a pretty good bet that the advertising expenditures are being wasted. For a restaurant promotion to be a success, more people have to come in, not the same or fewer.

Panels are somewhat difficult to put together, since they depend upon finding enough people in a given industry who are knowledgeable about a subject. We recommend that you create them if you can. We want you to know how they work, so we'll explain how we use panels at OTR.

4. Repeat experiences are critical. Having just gotten through explaining about promotions, you should know the obviousness of this rule. In order for you to know if the information you are collecting is valid, you have to go back to the same sources again and again. If you are looking at a particular McDonald's in a local mall, follow it constantly, through promotion and during nonpromotion times. Learn when the heaviest traffic is (usually breakfast and lunch, and especially weekends) and count the traffic then. Slower times just aren't important enough for you to waste your time.

If you are tracking sales of yogurt, check the same stores on the same days. (Monday morning, when stocks are most depleted, is the best time.) If you are tracking airline stocks, have the people in your panels looking at holiday and business traffic out of major airports on a regular basis.

The trick is to get into a regular rhythm of using the same people to look at the same information during the same intervals of time. Out of such behavior come identifiable patterns, and out of such patterns come the deviations that are the keys to making money in investing.

5. Send gifts and share information. At OTR, we go through a couple of thousand pounds of jelly beans, and even more Godiva chocolate every Christmas. We send small gifts and thank-you notes to the members of our panels for taking the time to share information with us. More important, we share information with panel members. It is standard procedure for us to tell all of the members of a panel about our findings. After our clients digest our reports, we send copies to our sources.

We do this for several reasons. The first is that it keeps people involved in the process, and makes them feel that they are part of a two-way exchange, instead of a one-way flow of information.

Second, it helps panel members to know whether they were part of the statistical majority, or part of the minority. Often, when a panel member's individual information is at odds with the information from the group as a whole, he or she will have an insight that accounts for the differences. This insight might be a regional preference. (For example, in snack foods, there is one dominant brand, Frito-Lay. But below that, the second brand varies by region, with no company dominating every region. Once you get to the No. 3 position in snack foods, the variance is even wider, with local brands predominating.) It might also be a special circumstance. (If you are tracking sunscreens, Seattle, with its notorious rainy weather and average of 315 days of clouds, mist, and rain per year, might not be the best place to look for sales trends. Florida, or Southern California would be places were you would be much more likely to spot an emerging trend in skin care.)

If you give your panel member a chance to think about it, he or she will probably come up with a reason that accounts for the differences.

When that happens, you have two alternatives. The first is to replace the panel member with someone whose experiences are similar to those of the majority, so that you gain additional statistical reinforcement. The second choice is to maintain the person as a member of your panel, precisely because his or her views are divergent but interesting. Divergent and interesting are important because they may point to future trends. If a panel member in California, reports experiences that are at odds with the group as a whole, you might have a new trend in the making, especially in fashion, food, or entertainment.

A third reason for sending thank-you notes and gifts is that panel members will give you access to something even more important than their own time. That is the time of other people. It is not uncommon for the people with whom our reporters are in contact to say, "I'm not the person you should be asking about that subject. But if you give Bob Smith at Acme a call, and tell him I said to call, he'll give you the real skinny on what is going on in the industry."

Sure enough, if you call Bob Smith and use your panel member's name, he will take your call, give you the information, and tell you to send regards to his friend, and ask him how his kids are doing. You have now brought a very important person into your regular circle, and all because you showed a little consideration.

6. Geographic breadth is important. The United States is a very big country. Not only does it have a large population—only China, India, and Russia have larger numbers of people within their borders—but it is geographically diverse. People are spread out all over the country, and where they live affects what they buy. You need to account for that geographic diversity in your reporting. You will need people in the key population centers. That means New York, Chicago, Los Angeles, Houston, Philadelphia and Florida (especially in the south of Florida—the Florida Panhandle has too few people). It probably also means someplace like Boston or Providence, and probably Atlanta, although Atlanta continues to be more representative of itself than of the South as a whole. The same thing is true for cities like St. Louis, Kansas City, and Seattle. They do not reflect the countryside surrounding them, the way, say, that Los Angeles and its suburbs are one, or New York and its suburbs are.

But you will also need some people from trend-setting areas. If you follow high-technology stocks, you need people from Silicon Valley—the area between San Jose and San Francisco—and from Austin and the suburbs of Washington, D.C., for starters, plus either Boston and New York. (Those five areas, according to the Industry Standard, accounted for about 60 percent of all the venture-capital spending in the United States in 1999 and 2000.)

If you are following the candy industry, you have to go to large-population centers because that's where the most candy is being consumed. There is a lot of common sense involved in geographic spread, but you do have to pay attention to the need for geographic diversity in creating your circle of information gatherers, and in creating panels. Remember: If you are doing marketplace checks by yourself, it is not going to be practical for you to develop such geographic diversity. Try, instead, to focus on companies that sell within a smaller area, like publicly traded regional firms.

7. Sample size is important. This seems too simple to need saying, but far too many people who read this are going to say to themselves, "If I call up a few people, I'll get the information I need." In statistics, there is something called a "confidence factor." Without going into how it is calculated, suffice it to say that the larger your sample is in relation to the entire body of people from which you are gathering information, the more reliable your information is likely to be.

What does that mean? Let us say that there are 2,000 people who buy candy for large chain stores, and for wholesale distributors who then resell to smaller stores. The entire universe of candy buyers is therefore 2,000 people. It is not all the people who go into a store to buy candy, but only the 2,000 folks who purchase candy in huge quantities for chain stores. If you know the purchasing behavior of this group, you know essentially everything there is to know about candy in the United States. The important question here is not how many candy buyers you speak with, but how much clout each buyer has.

Let's say, for example, that you speak with only five buyers, but one of them buys for Wal-Mart and another buys for Kmart. Between them, they probably account for 25 percent of all the bulk candy sold in America. Your other three buyers might account for another 1 percent! On the other hand, you might speak with a dozen buyers who collectively represent only 10 percent of the stores in the United States.

Which group is more statistically significant? Clearly the first group is, because it has more influence over the future sales of candy than the second group. Therefore, you need to pay attention not only to the number of people with whom you and your group speak, but the amount of buying they control.

8. Regularity of reporting is critical. Again, this seems to be pretty obvious, but if you want to make money using marketplace checks, regularity of reporting is really important. The way to see patterns emerge is to perform the same tasks at the same time every day or every week, the way a detective does surveillance. Chances are, your real life will throw up roadblocks to your ability to report, so choose times during the day or week when you know that you will have some time to devote to your marketplace-checking projects.

If you are working with a group, you will be its center, so you are also going to have to take the responsibility of prodding your people to do their interviews and to fill in their reporting sheets on a regular and timely basis. (More about that in Chapter 9.) Making money is like any other occupation. The more effort you put into it, the more reward you get out of it; so if people are beginning to slack off, you have to give them incentives to keep going. Making money ought to be incentive enough, but it is hard to be consistent on anything that is not your full-time occupation. In fact, most investment clubs fall apart after about three years because people don't put enough time into them, even when they are doing well.

If you are using an investment club or have enlisted a group of friends to help you with a marketplace-checking system, how do you get your people to keep up their good work? You need a combination of incentives. The same way that your group should get in the habit of sending thank-you notes and small gifts to their sources, you ought to be sending out little gifts and thank-you notes to your circle members. You also ought to get in the habit of talking to those people frequently. In the beginning of this book, we compared what you are doing to MCI's "friends and family" program, or Sprint's Nickel Nights. You probably ought to join a program like that to keep your costs down, and to encourage members to call each other. If your circle grows large enough, you might even want to look at getting your own 800 number, which will allow your members to call you at your expense.

9. Ask the same questions of the same people. We talked about the importance of this a little earlier, but I'd like to be a bit more definitive about this. By the same questions, I really mean the *same* questions, and not little variations on a theme. So, if the question is about dairy sales and you are talking to dairy buyers, the question to each buyer might be, "What is your percentage of sales from Land O' Lakes this month, compared to Kraft?" Or "Are you buying more from Kraft or Land O' Lakes? How much more?" Framing your questions carefully to get the most information in the shortest possible time ensures that you don't waste the valuable time of the people to whom you are talking. It also forces you to quickly put your information into a form that can later be translated into data that can be statistically manipulated.

Which brings us to our final point . . .

10. Hard data beats impressions every time. In marketplace checks, you are attempting to know—with some degree of certainty—the impact of sales on the future total revenues and profits of one company over another, so you'd better be spending as much of your time getting those sales numbers as possible, either as actual numbers or, better, as relative percentages. ("My sales were up 3 percent this week, and all of it went to Campbell Soup," reports a buyer in the soup category who represents 65 chain stores that purchase 5 percent of the soup in the United States. That's about as hard as you can get in the data field.)

Often, though, the buyers you speak with don't want to give you information that is so precise, because it may violate a company confidentiality agreement, or be considered a trade secret. When you run into that problem, you have to start calling around to try to find other sources of data. Or, if you have some data to begin with, you can use an impressionistic approach or a trade approach to get what you need.

Let's look at that soup buyer again. You call her up and she won't give you any numbers, but you already have some from a couple of other buyers. You say to her, "The general sense that I'm getting from the people I've spoken with is that Campbell's sales are up two or three percent. Are you having a similar experience?"

If she says yes, ask her if it is more or less than 3 percent and, if so, how much. This is a variant on the kids' game, "Twenty Questions," where, by asking questions of increasingly fine grain along a logical path, you will come to the answer you are looking for.

Even if all you get is impressionistic information, all is not lost. If your source is well qualified, those impressions are as valuable as hard data because they will point you in the right

101

direction. You have to learn, by experience, who is a good source and whose information is unreliable. Over time, as you get better and better people into your group, the quality of your information will go up, along with the quantity.

Do not expect to get the best information right from the start. Marketplace checking is a system that improves over time, as you gain more experience with it. Over the last five years, as our panels have developed and our reporters have become more knowledgeable about the industries and firms they cover, we have increased our accuracy in our finding of facts and our predictions. At some point this tops out—you can never reach 100 percent accuracy—but you will find that even if you increase your knowledge over the average investor only marginally, you will gain a tremendous advantage. No matter how small, a consistent advantage over the pack is worth a great deal. A racehorse that, after a mile and a half consistently beats the other horses by two feet is worth millions. The horse that, after the same run, is always a foot or two behind the pack is not worth entering in races.

One last note: I keep telling you to call people, but nearly all of the people you are going to call have real jobs, so they don't have much time to talk. In many cases, you will not reach them on the first try. Do not give up on them or relay your questions through voice mail. Tell them who you are and what you are researching, and tell them you are going to call back. Use your message to raise the awareness of the person you are calling about what you are doing. If you have not heard back within twenty-four hours, call again. Do not think that you are bothering the person you are calling. People will often put off something as long as they can; but if it is brought directly to their attention, they will address the issue. They might not be especially inclined to talk to you because they think they are too busy, but almost every person you call will contribute something if you are persistent.

Since we believe in being polite to people who help us, it makes sense to make the best use of a source's own staff. If a secretary or assistant answers, ask when the best time is for you to contact your source. Very early in the morning or late in the day are the times when most people don't have meetings. They may not even have their secretary in yet to screen their calls at these hours. Right before or after lunch may also be a good time to catch people.

For certain industries, some days are better than others. For example, supermarket buyers often schedule buying appointments on Tuesday, Wednesday, and Thursday, but not on Monday or Friday. As you get to know an industry, you will begin to get a sense of which days are best for doing research.

Once you have a good source on the line, you don't want to lose him or her—but it's very easy to do. Be sure to explain fully and accurately exactly what you're doing. Here's how:

- Because you do not have a conventional journalistic or Wall Street affiliation, you need to explain yourself to your contact. If you are a member of an investment group, you can identify yourself that way; but if you are an individual, here is what to say to sources who don't know you:

  "Hi, my name is Joe Smith, and I am doing some stock-market research. I am examining some general trends, so I don't use company or personal names of any sources for my reports. I wonder if you have a few moments to speak with me to discuss [name the topic here]."

- If your source asks how long the interview will take, you have nothing to gain by giving him or her the greatest amount of time it could take. Instead, you can say, "I can probably keep it to the amount of time you have available. Why don't we get started and you can tell me when you have to go." Alternatively, estimate five to fifteen minutes (depending upon the number of questions). This may sound short—but again, if anything, underestimate. If you know exactly what to ask and what is most important, you can make good use of a short amount of time. And if you and your source get into an interesting conversation on the trend, he or she may forget about the clock.

- Be prepared to fax or E-mail questions to some sources who will want to see exactly what you are asking before they answer. However, it is rare that you'll get your answers faxed back—it's usually better to suggest that you will call to get the answers verbally because the replies may bring up some additional questions.

- Some sources may feel more comfortable if they see some of your prior work. When you are first starting out, this will be hard; but as you begin to compile reports, be prepared to send them to sources, so they know that you are not just some oddball who is looking for a stock tip. You're not. Also, try to send them a report that pertains to their area of expertise, so they can see how thorough your group is.

- Respect your source's time as valuable. Don't stumble around or make small talk (unless your source seems to want to— then do so by all means). Tell him or her concisely what you are doing, and if your source is willing to go on, get right to the point. Which brings us to our most important point of all.

- Know exactly what you are going to ask, and what is most important. It's probably unwise to begin with a sensitive question like, "How are your store's sales this year?" Instead, start with a general nonoffensive question like, "How do you see consumer confidence this year?" This is really the first question, but in sheep's clothing. Generally, a retailer will tell you that consumer confidence is rising if sales are strong, or that it is falling if sales are weak. But once you get your subject going, get right to the point. You never know when your source will have to break off for

104

another call, so prioritize your questions. That way, if you get cut off, you already may well have covered the most important points.

- Finally, remember that these people are truly doing you a favor. If you treat your sources well the first time around, the next time you need to call, things will go much more smoothly.

7

FINDING THE UNUSUAL

Seeing the Forest,
the Trees, and the Path

In the last chapter, we talked about the need to look for patterns and anomalies. Patterns occur over and over, like people going to Burger King and McDonald's. Anomalies occur when people suddenly do things differently, like going to Subway. Sure, it's still fast food; but because McDonald's, Burger King, and Wendy's control such a large share of the fast-food market, even a small move—as small as a 1 percent shift—to another chain can mean a big improvement to the small chain's bottom line. When you begin to notice a break in what has been a long-established pattern, you and/or your team have to begin the process of investigation and reporting, and then of analyzing what that break means. When the break is even more pronounced, such as when people forsake all fast food altogether, and begin going to sit-down dinner restaurants, then you really have some news that translates into a big gainer.

Finding anomalies means learning how to see all over again. It means learning how to be naïve about what you see. In the 1984 film, *Moscow on the Hudson,* Robin Williams plays a member of the Moscow circus who comes to the United States and then defects. On his first day in an American supermarket, he walks down the coffee aisle and is confronted with so many choices that he faints from the emotional overload. That is a great example of being naïve about what you see. In order to really get a feel for what is going on in the supermarket—and hence, what is going on in the food industry—you must approach shopping as if it were a child's game. Do you remember being a kid and playing a game of spotting out-of-state license plates when you were traveling with your parents? Supermarket spotting is the same game, except that you are looking for new food items or, just as important, for rearrangements of old items. You have to walk through the supermarket asking yourself questions, and jotting down what you see.

If you are going to follow food-company stocks, for example, and you have a group, get them to agree to do their marketing on the same day every week. Ask people to choose different levels of supermarkets for their shopping. Supermarkets all seem to look the same, but in reality, they serve different economic and demographic groups. A grocery chain like Wegman's is generally geared to a very upmarket clientele, while a Sam's Club or a Costco or the German chain Aldi, which is big throughout the Midwest, focuses on value shoppers. In your own area, you undoubtedly know which chains serve which audiences; so when you are doing research yourself or putting together your group, figure out the best methods for getting the broadest kinds of coverage. Then go into the stores and begin the vital process of collecting information.

What do you see when you walk down a supermarket aisle? Are you looking at new products, or have you noticed that some of the brands that are available have relabeled their products? If so, why do you suppose the manufacturer did that? Often, a relabeling signals that the manufacturer is putting some marketing muscle behind the product; by putting a new label on it, the manufacturer wants you to notice the product. If it's the same old label, and you haven't been buying that brand, seeing it in a new "set of clothes" might get you to try the product. Combined with some couponing, that might be enough to win an extra point or two of market share.

New products fall into several categories: products that are wholly new, line extensions of existing products, size variations of existing products, products that have been around for a long time but that are new to your supermarket, and reformulated or repackaged existing products. Let's look at each in turn.

Products that are wholly new, such as Cool Whip, when it was first introduced decades ago, are quite rare. Cool Whip was the first nondairy whipped-dessert topping, and it was unlike anything else previously sold in the supermarket. Such unique products are rare, but they do pop up from time to time. Pay attention to them. The company that introduces them is taking a huge marketing gamble: that the novelty of the new will become a successful habit, leading to a market share large enough to justify the investment in a new product.

Bottled salsa is a great example of a wholly new product conquering a market. Twenty-five years ago, you could not find bottled salsa of any kind in a supermarket. American palates did not tolerate spicy foods well, and the condiment of choice was ketchup—preferably Heinz, which had a market share in excess of 80 percent. In fact, the dominance of Heinz ketchup, which was the company's largest-selling product, helped to make Heinz a food-marketing powerhouse. Then along came bottled salsas in the mid-1980s and, though it was not apparent at the time, salsa marked the end of Heinz's dominance in the condiment market.

By the mid-1990s, salsa sales had surpassed ketchup sales, and Heinz had missed the salsa boat. The growth of salsa was an easily observable trend, if you had been making marketplace checks on supermarkets all through the 1990s.

A more recent example is the new P&G product Fit, which is a wash designed to remove wax, dirt, and pesticide residue from fresh vegetables and fruits. Fit plays well to the growing concerns among Americans that the food chain is being imperiled. Fit is a product to watch because even though it would have only a small impact on P&G's bottom line, it could help change perceptions on Wall Street about the company and renew the idea that P&G is an innovative marketer.

Line extensions are another major way that companies attempt to grab market share. Supermarkets have fixed amounts of shelf space. The average supermarket carries about 40,000 items, and food, toiletries, and other packaged-goods companies introduce about 25,000 new items a year. This means that most of the new items have to be strong enough to displace something that is already selling in the supermarket, or in a drugstore or discount store. So packaged-goods marketers battle for existing shelf space by extending existing successful lines, in order to force the displacement of the goods of competitors.

One of the champions of line extensions is Coke. I can remember when there was just Coke and it came in glass bottles. In 1963 Coke added Tab as a diet drink. Then, in the 1980s, Coke began to add other related products and package them in an increasingly expanding number of containers. Now when you go down a supermarket aisle, you can choose from Coke, Diet Coke, Cherry Coke, and their caffeine-free related products. Meanwhile Pepsi also has produced multiple brands of its own. All these products take increasingly more space, leaving very little room for smaller regional brands. Is Caffeine-Free Diet Cherry Coke really needed? Are consumers thirsting for this product? Probably not. But if it keeps Dr. Brown's cherry soda off the shelves, then it is providing value to Coke's master plan to have you drink its product.

Therefore, when you are looking at products on the shelves, it also helps to know who is making them. One way to do that is simply to look at the label, but labels do not always divulge who the parent company is. To find that out, get yourself a copy of *Shopping for a Better World,* which is published annually by the Council on Economic Priorities. Although this guide is designed to help people make political choices about the products they buy—the theory is that consumers can reward or punish companies that do or don't follow socially responsible practices—the guide is a gold mine of information on all sorts of consumer products. It has virtually every brand of every category of product sold in supermarkets and chain stores, and its codes tell you who are the manufacturers behind the products, so you can keep a scorecard. For example, Hidden Valley Ranch salad dressings, a major brand, are made by the Clorox Company, whose main product is bleach. Tombstone Pizza? That's made by Philip Morris's Kraft division. As you can see, there's often no rhyme or reason, so the book is a good reference source.

The next categories—changes in size, or reformulated or repackaged goods—are very important classes of products. Often, they signal major changes in a company. For example, a couple of years ago, the average coffee can downsized from 16 to 10 ounces. Coffee consumption has been dropping in the United States for years, but coffee is still a large product category. So nearly all of the major coffee packers went to a smaller can at the same time.

By downsizing the weight inside the can but maintaining the can's size, manufacturers were able to do two things at once. First, they were able to maintain the absolute amount of physical shelf space devoted to coffee, which is important from a competitive perspective. Second, most manufacturers, such as General Foods, which packs Maxwell House, and Procter & Gamble, which packs Folger's coffee, did not lower the price for a can of coffee, in effect raising the price per pound of coffee, and with it, revenue per pound, by 60 percent. Coffee packers managed to turn a losing situation—declining coffee consumption—into a winning proposition.

When companies reformulate or repackage, they are doing much the same thing as when they shift size. Companies are always looking for an advantage, so when you see a company spend money on an existing product, you can be pretty sure that they have lost market share and are attempting to regain it. The mere fact of a reformulation or a repackaging ought to be a signal to you and your team to look deeper into a product category for clues about market-share changes, or about the existence of new market leaders. Often, a change will be made in response to a company that is not a market leader, and may not be on your radar screen, but which is taking sizable share away. Remember our toothpaste example? Church & Dwight still has only a small share of the toothpaste market, but its Arm & Hammer Baking Soda toothpaste has forced virtually every competitor to offer a baking-soda alternative just to blunt Church & Dwight's competition.

This should be a major lesson for you. When you are compiling your numbers on market share, it is easy to look at two or three market leaders and ignore the dozens—or even hundreds—of smaller brands that follow behind in the pack. But it is most often from those small brands that innovations come, and from which new trends emerge. More than twenty years ago, Silicon Valley marketing guru Regis McKenna (he's the man who designed the Apple Computer logo, among other things) wrote a much-quoted paper on the subject for the *Harvard Business Review,* titled "Marketing in the Age of Diversity." McKenna's thesis, which is even more true today, was that the real power in brands was the category labeled "other," rather than the dominant top two or three brands. In orange juice, ice cream, and a host of different categories, "other," meaning the nondominant brands, make up the majority of sales in the category. Therefore, watch what is going on amongst these lesser-known brands to find out what the large brands are going to be forced to do in order to maintain market share.

Finally, look out for products that have been in the marketplace for a long time but which are new to your own supermarket. These products indicate changes within your own community, and provide a distant-early-warning system of changes in taste, or even of demographics. These changes create opportunities for you if you can figure out what they mean. For example, if you see that your grocery store is suddenly carrying not one, but ten different brands of olive oil, and several different brands of balsamic vinegar, you can be certain that one of two things is happening: Either people are eating healthier, or they are eating more expensive fresh foods, prepared with more expensive cooking oil. (Olive oil is more than twice as expensive as corn oil.) Since most people attempt to control the amount of money they spend on food, a shift to more expensive cooking oil means that either people are spending more of their budgets on food, or that they have more dollars to spend. Either way, that means that other shifts will ripple through the community. Remember: Small changes are often indicators of hidden larger changes. If you can learn to identify the small changes through constantly making marketplace checks, you can begin to forecast the larger changes and, ultimately, their effects on the valuations of companies.

What we've just told you about supermarkets goes for every store. When you are looking at your community, you have to look at everything with naïve and curious eyes. If your neighbor is putting in a swimming pool, don't be envious! Take a drive around the neighborhood and see how many other people are putting in pools. You may notice that the number is significant, in which case you should begin to ask your group members to check out the swimming-pool situation in their own communities. In-ground swimming pools mean more concrete being poured, which means more work for cement plants, which ultimately means higher prices for cement-company stocks, if you can determine that there is a large enough uptick.

When you go into any store, learn to observe what people are buying. Look in other people's shopping carts. Observe what they are buying when you are on the checkout line. Anytime a new store opens in your neighborhood or community, visit it and look at the merchandise. Every store is an indicator of somebody's perceptions of the marketplace. If the owners are around, ask them why they opened their store. What trends did they observe that caused them to make a large investment in the future? If they have done their homework, their information is useful to you as well.

The process of looking for the unusual carries down to nearly everything you do. It means developing a curiosity about the world at large, down to what kind of toys your kids are playing with and what people are talking about at work. Learn how to become an observer, and then how to interpret what you've observed. Let's walk through some of the rules of becoming a trained observer, with some exercises that will help you sharpen your powers of observation.

1. Learn to see the forest, the trees, and the path. We've gone to a lot of trouble to tell you that everything is important, but that is a difficult concept. If you treat everything equally, how do you separate the truly important from the merely trivial? In the beginning, when you are teaching yourself the process of developing a marketplace-checking mentality, you don't. Nobody expects you to take this book and begin making money instantly. It's going to take you at least a couple of weeks of diligent practice before you can become adept enough at separating the important items from those of only passing interest, but you have to work on it. Start by making a list of all the possible sources of information with which you might come in contact every day.

Such a list might look like this:

Morning radio—news about the world, as well as commercials. What is being advertised? If you listen to radio or watch television, do you note a tremendous shift to or from dot-com advertising? The airways are clogged with one type of advertising. Note that some of the companies that are advertising are not the ones that were spending huge amounts in late 1999 and early 2000, before dot-com stocks crashed. The companies that are still spending are worth a serious look because they are more likely to be the winners. This information is already reflected in stock prices, but there are many more dot-com companies being advertised than there are dot-coms that are already public. Which of the new ones will be the companies that grow? Make some notes.

Off to the bathroom. What kinds of soap, cosmetics, toilet paper, and skin-care products do you use? Where did you buy your towels and washcloths? Do you know the products that other people use? Do you purchase the same brands over and over, or do you try new brands? What about other people you know? Learn to begin asking people about such things, and when you visit people in their homes, learn to look at labels. When you see something new, don't be afraid to ask where it was purchased. (You don't need to know the purchase price. You're inquisitive, not gauche.)

Examine your own closet while you are getting dressed. Where do *you* buy your clothes? Is it in a department store, a specialty chain like The Gap or Banana Republic or The Limited, or in a boutique. Do you think you spend more or less than people of your age and income on clothes? Learn to be curious about the clothes that people wear, and to notice when people are making a shift from one style to another. It might begin to tell you something. For example, I noticed recently, on a business trip to and from San Francisco, that about 60 percent of the people—men and women—were wearing jeans, even though

115

khakis and other dress pants have supposedly supplanted jeans in the minds of the American consumer. We will be looking at this seeming upsurge in jeans and what it might portend.

Now you go into your kitchen to grab a bite to eat. What is in your refrigerator? Again, learn to look at brands and sizes, and begin to measure what you are consuming against what is being consumed by people you know. When you ask questions, you are looking for patterns and variances. Try to get a few people you know to list everything they've eaten for a week, just as a small research project. Tell people that you are doing some marketplace research on eating habits, to see if there are any new trends emerging, such as cereal for dinner.

It's time to head off to work. If you are like the vast majority of Americans, you are going to commute alone, in your car. There are more than 150 brands and models of automobile on the American road. Can you tell one car from another quickly? Can you tell new cars from old cars? If you can, then make it a point to count and classify every car on the road as you go to work every day, until a pattern begins to emerge.

The same thing is true whenever you drive. If you go to your local mall, for example, and you see that there are an unusual number of Dodge Durangos in the lot, that might mean something. You know that the Durango is a relatively new car, so if you see lots of them, you are either looking at an anomaly—lots of people with Durangos have decided to go to your shopping mall on this particular day, or something is afoot.

Next, confirm your observations. Keep a count of the Durangos you see over the next couple of days, and look at the license-plate holders that the dealers provide so you can determine if the cars you are seeing are local or if they're being bought out of town. Most people buy their cars within a fifty-mile radius of their homes; so if you are seeing a lot of locally purchased Durangos, then you definitely know that there is something going on.

Now you have to develop a theory. Does the presence of lots of Durangos mean that Dodge is selling more cars than expected? Does it mean that your community has developed a small pocket of prosperity? Does it mean that a lot of people are taking advantage of a great lease deal? You're going to have to test out all of those theories.

Start by going to the local Dodge dealer, looking at the cars, and talking to the salesmen all the while. Ask them why they think sales are suddenly up, and ask them how their sales are stacking up against national sales. Ask them if there has been a change in the kind of customer who has been walking through the door recently, or is it part of some larger trend they see. If you want information, you have to dig for it.

Once you have some information, you have to test its relevance. Go to a couple of other Dodge dealers in the area. Ask the same questions while you are looking at cars. Then go to the library, or onto the Internet, and get some company data on DaimlerChrysler, the parent company of Dodge. Find out how the stock has performed over the past two or three years, versus its sales. Is the information you are developing being reflected in the price? If not, you have a potentially sound stock purchase.

That's what marketplace checks are all about: looking for the unusual, and then developing enough information to shape a theory about what your unusual observation actually means. Right now you may be thinking that it is impossible to notice the type of cars that are being driven and how they are changing. It's not impossible, but gradual change is difficult to spot. Look at pictures you have, or a movie or a TV show from the 1970s. Look at the cars. Now go for a drive. Immediately you notice that twenty years ago there were no minivans, no SUVs, but plenty of station wagons. At some time there was a change, and suddenly there were plenty of SUVs and minivans, but almost no station wagons. If you had noticed early, you could have

117

invested in Chrysler and done very well. The trick is to see change early. It is difficult, and it takes practice, but it can be done.

Continue through your day. You decide to go to the movies in the evening. You've read in the newspaper or *Entertainment Weekly* that the movie you are watching is in its second week of release, and that it is No. 1 at the box office, but you notice that the theater is empty. What do you do? You make some phone calls to people you know and ask people how heavily attended the movie was in their own towns and cities. Maybe you find that what you've noticed in your own theater is an anomaly— after all, tastes vary from community to community.

But if many people report the same thing, then you know that the movie has no "legs" or staying power, and that it will drop way down the list very quickly. Check the stock pages to see if the film's first-week gross gave the studio's stock a lift. If so, you can bet that a poor second-week showing will send the stock back down, giving you an opportunity for a quick short sale.

And so off to bed. What kind of mattress are you sleeping on? How new is it? Do you know how often Americans replace their mattresses, or what the trends in mattresses are? No? That's too bad, because there are some very interesting trends, to thicker, more expensive sleep-support systems. Now people often spend more than $1,000 for a mattress, so the companies that make them are becoming more profitable on a per-unit basis, even though the absolute number of mattresses sold in the United States rises only slowly each year. In fact, mattresses are like cars. There are endless models and brands, but only a very few manufacturers, and the trends are toward rising average costs. If you know that, you can get more than a good night's sleep on your knowledge. You can make some money.

2. Now that you've begun to look at everything, learn to look at one thing in depth. Once you get into the habit of becoming curious about the world at large, it is time to become obsessed with one particular thing. If you are working with a group and have set up a panel, you and your team ought to sit down and narrow your list, so you can begin the process of becoming enough of an expert that you can feel confident about asking questions of the *real* experts on your panels, and of being able to draw conclusions from what you've been told.

If you are doing this alone, the process is the same. Focus on one element that looks most important, and begin to contact experts you know in the area. How do you decide which subject areas to pick? It will likely depend upon three things: how much you want to trade, how much news the sector generates, and the ratio of small companies to large companies in the sector.

Here is why each is important. As we've said, you can make money in any sector, on almost any stock, if you know enough about it, and regularly know more than anybody else. That knowledge influences both buy and sell decisions. As your knowledge changes, you may constantly and repeatedly be buying and selling the same stocks. That is what day traders do, except that they are buying and selling very fast and frequently, upon perceived momentum. You could buy and sell a single stock or a couple of stocks in a sector over and over again—not with the frequency of day traders, to be sure, but often enough to catch much of the cyclical nature of the stocks in the group.

This is especially true for sectors that have natural, predictable cycles, like retailing. If you look at the history of retail stocks, you'll see that they follow the economy, with the exception of Christmas. The Christmas selling season accounts for almost two-thirds of all sales and almost all the profits of the average retailer, so retail stocks track quarter-to-quarter sales growth for most of the year, and year over year profit growth in the Christmas quarter, since as the Christmas quarter goes, so goes the company for the entire year. If you follow the economy, follow the sector, and track your own stocks carefully through marketplace checks, you'll have remarkably good information about how each quarter is shaping up, before anyone else does.

How much news the sector generates is also critical. There is a constant battle for what is called "share of mind." That is what you pay attention to, and news is one of the things that people give their regular attention. Companies that generate a lot of news generate a higher share of mind than companies that generate little news; a company like Microsoft, which is constantly in the news, has more active stock trading than a company like Kafus Industries (a company that makes environmentally responsible processed building materials), which generates relatively little news.

Stock prices rise and fall not only on the perceptions that news generates, but on the sheer volume of news as well. If there is little news about a company, Wall Street's own analysts begin to believe that the company is unimportant, and spend less time covering the company within its own segment. This is good for you because it allows an information disequilibrium buildup, and that spells opportunity for the savvy marketplace checker. If you know that an ignored company's revenues and profits are on the rise, and nobody else is paying attention, you have the opportunity to buy low and sell high. If there is too much information about a company, many people are probably covering its every move, so the chances that you will discover something unique are lessened.

A good example is Closure Medical Corporation, a highflier when it first introduced its Dermabond skin adhesive as an alternative to sutures in mid-1998. Originally, the product was marketed to surgeons and, because of that, it came up against the dominance of Johnson & Johnson's Ortho group. As a result, the stock crashed, and analysts essentially wrote it off and the stock fell from a high of nearly 70 to around 15. But then the company began marketing the adhesive to emergency-room physicians, where it found a home because it is a good alternative to stitches for small wounds on the faces of children. We told our subscribers in June 1999 that about 15 percent of ER doctors were using Dermabond, and that the product had met with general approval. The stock began climbing, and is now selling around 32, a 113 percent gain.

Of course, as we said in Chapter 1, news is not always truth. With the rise of the Internet, there is a tremendous amount of half-truth floating around, not to mention outright lies. Noted computer-industry consultant Esther Dyson addressed that subject in an essay titled "End of the Official Story":

> The Net is a medium not for propaganda, but for conspiracy. Conspiracies can reveal the truth in a world of oppression, or spread misinformation among cranks who shut out the truth. The difference is hard to distinguish. Examples of conspiracy on the Net are well-known. A few years ago, Intel had a flaw in one of its chips that was discovered by a math professor who told others about it. Intel tried to downplay the problem. After all, which seems more serious: a minor bug or a secret error that a multibillion-dollar company is trying to cover up? Learning the answer cost Intel half a billion dollars. (Intel now has an active "two-way" Net-based communication channel with customers.)

Your job as a marketplace checker is to pierce through the tangle of half-truths and rumors, to find real information that will help you make money. But sometimes half-truths contain just enough information that, with a reliable information-gathering system, you can find out the real facts, and then convert those into insights.

Finally, the ratio of small companies to large ones within a sector is very important. You are looking for sectors, like medical instrumentation and electricity generation, where there are many small players, and where the industry has not yet gone through much consolidation, for two reasons. First, at some point, the economics of the industry will force consolidation, and then a wave of mergers and acquisitions will sweep across the sector landscape like a tsunami, taking everything in its path. At that point, the first companies to make an acquisition will probably underpay for the company being acquired. The second company will probably pay something close to fair market value. But once the takeover race begins, everyone else will overpay, and that's where your opportunity to make money arises. The more companies you own that are taken over, the more money you will probably make.

When a sector has many small players and a few large ones, it is likely to have many pure plays. We said earlier that pure-play companies—those which had only a narrow product line—were easier to track than companies that made many products or owned many divisions. It is clearer when a pure-play company does something right, and much more obvious when it makes a mistake. A good example of how both forces come into play was U.S. Surgical, the company that developed the surgical stapling machine. For years, the company and its stock enjoyed tremendous growth because the company essentially had a monopoly on its product. From a start-up in the late 1960s, U.S. Surgical grew into a good-sized company, a mid-cap with annual sales of about $1 billion at its peak.

But beginning in the late 1980s, Johnson & Johnson (J&J) began making its own staplers and other instruments that competed with U.S. Surgical's. For a while, U.S. Surgical simply outcompeted J&J with newer and better technology, and maintained the price premium it was able to charge.

Then—gradually—J&J was able to outmaneuver U.S. Surgical, and the company's fortunes began to wane. During the mid-1990s, the company actually lost money for the first time in thirty years, and only the heroic efforts of the company's founder, Leon Hirsch, and his employees, kept the company from disaster.

Finally, by about 1998, they managed to turn the company around and make it profitable again. But then along came Tyco Industries, which offered a nice premium for U.S. Surgical stock, and the company passed into history.

3. Bring in outside sources. When I was telling you about my early days, one of the things I said was that I read a lot of magazines. I still do. I can't be everywhere and I can't look everywhere, and neither can you. The professional journalists who write for and edit these magazines are like an army of trained personal observers for you. Every single industry has a hierarchy of news, and if you decide to focus upon a particular sector, learning all of the news sources that the sector has to offer will help you.

Begin with government sources. The U.S. Department of Commerce has hundreds of experts whose sole job it is to collect data on products manufactured in the United States. The Department of Agriculture has hundreds of experts who do nothing but specialize in single crops, like lemons or wheat. The Food & Drug Administration and the National Institutes of Health can tell you what is going on in the pharmaceutical industry, and the Treasury Department and the Securities and Exchange Commission can tell you what is going on in financial services. Their knowledge is invaluable because it can serve as a foundation for building an information base upon which your marketplace-check system will work.

There are a number of different ways to access Washington-based research. The first is through the *Statistical Abstract of the United States,* which is available both in book and CD-ROM form. It is filled with charts and tables on every conceivable subject, beginning with demographics, and going through consumption and spending habits.

To access Washington's legion of government researchers, buy a copy of *Who Knows What: A Guide to Experts,* published by Washington Researchers, Ltd. They also periodically publish a book devoted solely to Washington experts, but *Who Knows What* will provide almost everything you need. The company also publishes *State Sources of Company Intelligence,* if you are looking for information on companies in greater depth, since companies have to file more information with the states in which they are incorporated. It also issues two interesting books about company research: *How Competitors Learn Your Company's Secrets,* which will give you many useful tips on doing research, and *How to Find Information About Divisions, Subsidiaries and Products.* This is a really useful book if you decide that you want to tackle some of the large multiproduct, multidivision companies that are increasingly common, like Sara Lee, Tyco, Eastman Kodak, or P&G.

Once you have the basics covered, look at how companies fit into their own industry groups. Go to the library and examine the *Encyclopedia of Associations.* Industry associations often start out with the same government statistics for their own databases, but then add lots of information from their members that is available nowhere else. Much of this information is published on a regular basis, so, for example, if you are covering Home Depot and Lowe's, you can go to the National Home Improvement Association, the National Lumber Association, or a number of other associations, and pick up reams of data on how much drywall is being sold, or trends in kitchen remodeling, or other useful information. Industry groups also have their own experts, and that is where they are most useful. When you are doing panels, they are good people to consult for names, the "who should I be talking to" kinds of questions that will help you avoid spinning your wheels. Many of the associations also publish free newsletters, and sponsor conferences. You don't have to actually go to the conferences, but you can look at names on conference and seminar proceedings, and get some additional sources.

While we are on the subject of conferences, let's talk about them and trade shows for a bit. Just as every industry has associations, they also have conferences and trade shows. If you really want to know what is going on within an industry group, what the trends are, you ought to make it your habit to go to at least one large trade show per year. If you are investing, you can often deduct the cost of going to the show as research, and you can add a little extra time to it and get a bit of vacation in as well.

If you want to follow the food industry, the International Food Exhibition is the place to be. Every single major and minor food manufacturer and packer is there, with booths and displays, and plenty of new products for you to taste. More important, every buyer from every grocery chain is also there, along with thousands of wholesalers. All of those people make it their business to know what the trends in food are going to be. Make it *your* business to get to know them.

The next step up in the information chain is specialized newsletters. These are often expensive, private-source publications that are read by industry analysts on Wall Street and by government regulators. One of the largest publishers of these specialized newsletters is Phillips Publishing, which is located in Potomac, Maryland, and which specializes in many of the defense, electronics, and aerospace industries, but also closely follows the multitude of Washington regulatory agencies. How do you find these often-arcane newsletters? You ask the experts to whom you are talking what they read, especially what specialized publications. They are not worried that you are ever going to become expert enough in their fields to take away their jobs, so they won't hesitate to tell you where they get their information. Again, don't forget to send a thank-you note whenever you get really useful information.

Following the information ladder up to its next rung takes you to the realm of trade magazines and newspapers. Again, go to the library and look through a copy of *Bacon's Magazine Directory,* or a set of SRDs (Standard Rate and Data guides), which are organized by industry. These will tell you who publishes the magazines, how much they cost (many are free if you are in the trade or industry, or are an industry "analyst"), the editorial staff, along with useful phone numbers. Once again, you should subscribe to the key publications in the industry you are researching. One of the reasons for talking to industry experts is the proliferation of trade magazines. At least one of them is the "bible" of the industry—in depth, authoritative and well-researched and reported, while the others are just a waste of time. Get to know the good from the bad, and stay with the good.

A great way to find publications and industry information is to spend an hour or two on the Internet with a good search engine. If you want to know about the cement industry, search for "cement." If that does not work, try "construction." Try the names of a cement company. Eventually you will find even the most obscure publication.

Another source is the industry conventions. Specialty magazines always have a booth or exhibit at their industry's trade shows, and often sponsor them. You can usually pick up free copies of their latest issues, as well as get a "conference-special subscription discount." At OTR, we subscribe to over 250 of these magazines.

Ranking higher than trade publications are specialized "enthusiast" magazines and specialty national magazines. *Rolling Stone* and *Spin* are examples of good enthusiast magazines for the record industry. They are of more general interest than *Billboard* or *Cashbox,* which cover the record industry from a dollars-and-cents perspective, or *Variety,* which covers the entertainment industry. If you read both types of magazines, you'll be able to come up with a very good sense of what people in the industry are thinking, as well as what new projects are coming up. Similarly, you might read *Gourmet* magazine to discover the latest trends in upscale dining, but you would read *Restaurant Business* to find out what the latest trends in the dining industry are. In *Restaurant Business,* there is a constant assessment of how the public is responding to new initiatives by restaurateurs and companies in the restaurant business, measured by sales volumes and average check size. In *Gourmet,* the question is, "Is the food any good?" Based on the reviews to the latter questions, for upscale restaurants such as Wolfgang Puck's Spago, a company will develop a large concept restaurant like California Pizza Kitchen, to cash in on the gourmet-pizza trend for a larger audience.

At the top of the information pyramid are the national media and, for the most part, they are the least useful. Nearly two decades ago, John Naisbitt wrote *Megatrends,* a book about the forces that were supposed to shape our lives in the future. Much of what Naisbitt wrote was inaccurate, but one of the things he was correct about was the place of newspapers, television and national magazines. Naisbitt said that those media outlets are always the last to know something, and almost never the first.

Why is that? Naisbitt's explanation was that because the national media have little space, they tend not to waste it on stories of only passing interest. They wait until a trend is well confirmed and then write about it, explaining and giving significance to what everyone is already talking about. They are simply sounding boards for the conventional wisdom.

Remember: All of these data and information sources are not a substitute for marketplace checking. They are designed to help give you a broader base of knowledge, or to put you in touch with experts who can give you better information, or to widen and deepen your perspective on the industries or companies that you follow. With some of this knowledge, you will begin to understand the things that you are seeing, and begin to make some informed judgments about whether things that you see are worth following up with additional inquiry. The most important asset you posses is your time. You don't want to waste it chasing down every rumor or meaningless tidbit of information. The better you can prepare yourself by using outside sources such as the ones we've listed above, the more likely it is that you will make better choices in the pursuit of moneymaking knowledge in the marketplace.

Now that I've given you a lot of sources, what do you do with them? Aside from asking your questions, ask for more sources. If you speak with a magazine editor or analyst, ask for referrals. Ask the referrals for additional sources. Ask the people you talk to at companies for the names of people in their regional or national headquarters. You are creating a chain of value for yourself, so you have to keep extending it.

Also, there is an interesting thing about information called the Circularity Rule: If you ask enough people for information, eventually the last person you speak with will refer you to the first person who began the chain. At that point, you have exhausted all of the known sources, and your information chain is completed.

Besides asking people, how do you get more sources? Learn to mine the Internet. When you speak to sources, get their E-mail addresses as well as their phone and fax numbers. In many companies, an E-mail address can gain you access to a company directory, which can give you more names, addresses and, more important, titles.

Also, use the Internet to get at sources sideways. If you can't get to a company directly, go to a college or university business school in the company's hometown. Many of the professors in the marketing department will be doing some sort of consulting for the company. Even if they won't give you direct information, they will give you names of people you can call.

They will also be able to open up an entire additional network of information: academic research. There are numerous journals where academics publish their papers, and all of them are fodder for names. Once you have the journal names, look up the indices on the Internet, and look for names in subject areas that interest you.

What else can sources do for you besides answering your questions? Remember: These people are experts in their own fields, so if you show interest in what they are doing, they may mentor you. Ask them what questions you ought to be asking, or what key issues you ought to be keeping your eye on. For example, ask questions about changes in distribution channels, since those are often the first places where major changes in the way products are sold—and to whom—first appear.

While you are at it, provide referrals to other sources. You don't want information flowing only to you, but rather, back and forth among your team members and your panel members. For example, if you are covering the camera industry, you are also going to be covering the film and battery industries as well, since they are closely related. If you have a good camera source with good insights, suggest to the people you speak with about batteries that they talk with your source as well. If you have written a report for your battery team, give it to the film and camera people, too.

Sources can also save you time. You are coming at an industry from the outside; or, even if you are an insider, as an amateur. But a real insider makes the best use of his or her time. He or she goes only to the most productive trade shows, and reads only the best, most knowledgeable publications. If your source will share that wisdom, collected carefully over a lifetime of work, you have developed a very good source, indeed.

Your sources can also act as a sounding board. Often, when new trends begin to emerge, talk to your best sources first. These people will help you discern new patterns, sometimes even before you do. If you have uncovered a fact that appears to be an anomaly, bringing it to the attention of a good source before you begin to attempt to chase it down can save a lot of heartache.

Finally, a little common sense is in order. Sources are people, and that means they are imperfect sometimes. They might give you bad information, and sometimes they are under outside stresses. If you can do something for a source to ease a burden—in the context of passing on information—do it willingly. You will be helping a valuable asset, and it won't cost you anything to do a favor that will be appreciated.

8

OBSERVE THE EVERYDAY

Invest in What You Know

I've been talking to you about viewing the world as a sea of data, but what you probably need now is an example. Walk with me around my own neighborhood in San Francisco. We'll look at a number of things, and I'll explain their significance, starting from the moment I walk out the door.

Literally the first thing I see when I come down the steps of my house is a portable toilet. When I was writing this book, I was having work done on my house. My neighborhood was built in the 1920s and, like a lot of neighborhoods, it has had its ups and downs. Right now it is on an upswing again, with lots of young professionals moving into the area. Even if I never spoke to my neighbors, I'd know that, because in addition to the portable toilet outside my house, I can stand on the corner and look in any direction and count about six more johns. That's a sign that the neighborhood is going through a serious remodeling spree, and that means lots of sales of wallboard, lumber, wiring, plumbing fixtures, paint, and wallpaper, not to mention new furniture and accessories. As I drive around the neighborhood, on my way to the main shopping street, I make a note to

131

check out companies like Home Depot, Masco, Lowe's, Kohler, and others related to either home remodeling or furnishings. If there is a lot of remodeling activity going on in one neighborhood, that's not news; but if it's going on across the country, it will be reflected in the stock prices of the remodeling companies. Sure enough, it is, and 2000 continues to be a good year for home stores and home furnishings companies.

When I get up to the corner, I make a right, and I'm on the main shopping street of my neighborhood. A couple of years ago, most of the stores on the street were local stores, small boutiques, and hardware and food stores without any connection to national chains. Big national chains had long abandoned Main Streets in favor of shopping malls, but my little shopping area has been undergoing a renaissance recently.

There is the obvious Starbucks, which has run counter to the trend and locates most of its stores in cities. San Francisco seems to have a Starbucks on nearly every corner, but the one in my neighborhood is special. It is larger than the average Starbucks, and the company uses it to test new menu items. People are spending more time in their stores, and in San Francisco, at least, the neighborhood Starbucks has become a kind of office away from the office for many start-up companies. You see lots of people at tables, working from their laptop computers, and those people are there for a couple of hours at a time. So I'm going to find out if my neighborhood observations are part of a broader trend. Is what I see in this Starbucks also the case in other San Francisco neighborhoods, and in other cities? If so, what might it mean to investors?

Right down the street from Starbucks is a Wells Fargo cash machine. It is the most heavily used cash machine in the area, and the local Wells Fargo Bank is the most popular bank with consumers. I watch bank traffic, and I know that Wells Fargo has made a huge effort to attract customers by providing a lot more services to its customers than any of its competitors. Aside from offering free ATM usage, you can use the ATM to pay bills, or make deposits, or many other things you use your money or other accounts for. The bank itself has longer hours than any other bank in the neighborhood, and it has good weekend hours as well. Since everyone around here works so hard, and works so many hours, having a bank that is open in the evenings is an advantage for the people who live in the neighborhood.

As we move up the street, the next store we're going to stop into is the local Walgreen's. It is one of my favorite stores because it is a microcosm of retailing. A Walgreen's drugstore, or a Rite-Aid or an Eckerd, or any of the chain drugstores, is more than just a drugstore. It is a convenience store for people who are too time pressed to shop in a supermarket. As a result, its limited shelf space is an accurate reflection of what people need most or are buying most. If an item does not move off the shelves, it is gone very quickly, and is replaced by something that will sell faster. In addition, the store carries several brands of each hot-selling item; so by looking at how much has already been bought—the relative depth of products hanging or stacked on the shelf—you have a handy reference about the comparative strength of one brand over another.

When you first come into the store, almost the first thing you see are batteries. People use a lot of batteries. Kids' toys, radios, personal tape and CD players, cameras, and flashlights all use up a lot of batteries. I look at the battery display rack, and I can immediately see that the Duracell batteries are selling the best, followed by the Kodak batteries, and then the Eveready. This is out of the normal order of things because Duracell and Eveready are the two leading brands, and Kodak hardly advertises at all. Since batteries are commodity products that require heavy advertising, brands that are selling well without advertising are cash cows for their manufacturers and drive more revenue to the bottom line. Batteries might not be ultimately material to Kodak's bottom line—the volume may be too small—but it might force you to look past the company's reliance on photographic film.

I make a left turn down the first aisle, and there are bottled waters and sports drinks like Gatorade. I look not only at the items that are on eye level, but I look at the items that are on the lower shelves as well. Stores place their best-sellers at eye level in order to move more merchandise, so it becomes a challenge for packaged-goods manufacturers to get the right shelf position for their wares. In large supermarkets, where the company reps stack the shelves, it is common to see a rep rearranging the shelves to give his or her own products more space; but in a Walgreen's, the store clerks stack the shelves, and you know that the manager is looking at the daily and weekly computer printouts to make his decisions. On the bottom shelves are the items in a category that are moving most slowly, the ones that will probably be replaced with newer products before too long. Think of a chain drugstore as a retail laboratory, where products prove themselves before they take on the larger shelf-space wars of the supermarkets and discount stores.

Right beyond the bottled waters is the candy aisle. This is one of my favorites because Americans are a nation of candy eaters, and there are relatively few manufacturers. It was by looking in my local Walgreen's that I first noticed the absence of Hershey candy during the 1999 Halloween preseason. A check of stores around the country led me to the fact that Hershey had installed a huge new computer inventory-tracking and manufacturing-resource program, and that they were having problems with it. Those problems made it all but impossible for Hershey to ship during the single biggest candy season of the year. Next to the candy is chewing gum, another large category, and here I notice that Arm & Hammer has a new chewing gum that is designed to clean your teeth. This gum also turns up in the aisle with toothpastes and toothbrushes and dental floss, so I know that the company is putting a big push behind it as a new product. It will be interesting to track the sales of this gum. Will it generate competitors, or is it just a passing fad?

There are many more aisles in Walgreens, but this gives you an idea of how observations in an ordinary convenience/drugstore can help you form a coherent picture of neighborhood trends.

Now out the door and to the right we go, continuing up the street. There is both a Gymboree and a Baby Gap, and both stores are essentially deserted, even though this is a Saturday. Once, not so long ago, both were mobbed; but as the children in the neighborhood have grown up, they have grown past the clothes sold by these two retailers. Moreover, the Gymboree line has been static for a while. It still emphasizes the same bright crayon colors: red, yellow, green, and blue. In American society, there is always a restless search for the next new thing; and what looked fresh five years ago now looks old and tired. So both retailers are lagging, which leads me to make a note to find out how both are doing nationwide.

Farther up the street is a fancy wine shop that has a sign in the window advertising an opening for a cheese expert. As I mentioned earlier, San Franciscans have long been comfortable with wine. This is a big wine-growing region. But cheese and crusty breads are beginning to expand their presence. There are a couple of good local bakeries that make sourdough bread, but the neighborhood is beginning to see the emergence of peasant breads of various nationalities.

What else do I see on the street? Not one, but two retail brokerage firms are in the process of opening offices. This is a sure sign of the growing prosperity of the neighborhood, both of the people who have moved in and of the older people who already live here. Stockbrokers are among the savviest people when it comes to money. It's their business, and they will open a retail office only where they know it will support a level of deposits and investment to keep a small army of commission-generating stockbrokers happy and well fed.

Now I walk back to my house and get into my car. I am going on a short trip downhill to the Marina, where I shop at the Safeway. The Marina Safeway is no different from any other supermarket. It has all of the food and nonfood items that supermarkets have, but it is, in its own way, a completely different take on what is selling and what is not. In supermarkets, traditionally, the deli section is nearest the front door, to grab you before you set out down the aisles, and sell you those oh-so-expensive impulse purchases, the foods that are freshly prepared and have the best smells.

This Safeway is no different. There, in between the front of the store and the deli counter, is a wagon piled high with fresh-baked crusty bread, cheeses, and different Italian salamis and hard sausages. Cheeses and fresh bread in two completely different places tells me that what I see in my neighborhood is not just a local phenomenon, and that there is almost surely a trend in the making. As far as I know, all of these imported cheeses are handled by small importers, but perhaps some large company has spotted the trend and is moving in to take advantage of it.

Down the first aisle are fresh fruits and vegetables. There is nothing special here. Safeway has a good selection of produce and, in the past decade, the varieties and kinds of produce have expanded greatly. There are half a dozen different kinds of tomatoes, a half dozen different varieties of apples, depending upon the season, lots of different kinds of fresh mushrooms.

That's pretty recent. It used to be that all you could get were button mushrooms. Now you can get creminis and portobellos, and even oyster mushrooms now and then. The move to more upscale mushrooms means that tastes are growing more sophisticated, and that people are willing to spend more on food.

Both of those trends bode well for the food industry. Supermarket margins are extremely low, so each time a supermarket chain can substitute a high-margin item for a low-margin one, it is going to make just a little more money. Moreover, as people fill their shopping baskets with more expensive foods, the supermarket makes more money because those items are generally not couponed.

Making the first turn from the produce section, we come upon the freezer cases and chilled milk and juice products. I always look there because both industries are low-barrier-of-entry businesses that attract new entrants all the time. There are a couple of new brands, and a few brands that are missing. I make notes and move on down the snack-food aisle.

Snack foods are an interesting category. One company, Frito-Lay (a division of Pepsico), has a dominant share, and all of the rest of the snack-food producers are also-rans. Therefore, when you are looking at pretzels, popcorn, potato chips, corn chips, tortilla chips, and other kinds of chips, you are really looking for trends. Have tortilla chips crowded popcorns off the shelf? What kind of popcorn is selling? Are they the highly buttered versions, or is it the no-butter version? What does this tell you about the people who are buying at this store? More important, what does it tell you about the value of the smaller companies. If you see Snyder's of Hanover, a local Pennsylvania brand, or Utz, a Maryland brand, suddenly turning up nationwide, they are doing it at the expense of Frito-Lay's shelf space. Those become mid-cap opportunities.

On past the snack foods to the "health foods." Once upon a time, Safeway had a large health-foods and organic section, but no more. Does this mean that people have given up on organic and healthy foods? Not at all. What you notice as you go up and down the aisle is that the healthy or organic brand has been incorporated next to the regular brands, so that it is now considered to be such a large part of the market that this store, at least, does not need a special section. This means that people can choose which organic and healthy products they want to buy, and that mirrors today's "mix and match" society. Very few people are dedicated to any one way of doing things. They take a little from Column A and a little from Column B. It makes life a lot harder on marketers, who would prefer to fit people into neat little demographic and psychographic boxes, but Americans just aren't like that anymore.

That's yet another reason why you need to become a marketplace checker. The standard types of data that packaged-goods companies relied upon no longer provide all of the answers. In fact, they provide very few answers, except among older demographic groups. As the number of young people moving into the adult population continues to increase—the leading edge of the "Baby on Board" generation—that is, kids born after 1985—are now fifteen, and beginning to come into their prime spending years, first as teenagers with lots of discretionary income, and within five years, as young adults. They not only buy different things, but they buy it in different ways. They are just as likely to purchase over the Internet, or go to a giant warehouse store, as to go to a conventional supermarket or drugstore.

Aside from the organic and health-food insight, and the bread and cheese in the deli section, there is not much of interest in the Safeway today, so I jump back into my car and drive back uphill to Trader Joe's. Trader Joe's is to California what Whole Foods Market is to the East Coast: a small chain of upscale grocery stores that specializes in organic produce, fresh fish and meats, interesting cheeses, whole grains, and the cosmetics and toiletries of small manufacturers who feature lots of natural ingredients. I like to wander around Trader Joe's and look in the shopping baskets of people, to see what they are buying, as much as I like looking for new and unusual things myself.

One of the processes you go through as you develop your marketplace-checking skills is sizing up people. Trader Joe's is at the edge of several neighborhoods, so virtually everyone in the store came by car. Most of the cars in the parking lot are fairly upscale. I don't necessarily mean Mercedes and BMWs, although there are a good number of those, but Volkswagen Passats instead of Beetles, and V-6 Toyota Camrys instead of the four-cylinder models. When you look at those cars, and then at the record sales numbers that automakers have been posting for the last few years, it is little wonder that automobile-company profits have been at record levels. But when you go inside Trader Joe's, and try to match the cars to the people, that is when the real fun begins. There's no easy way to make the matches work. The crowd is predominantly young, and predominantly casually dressed, in jeans, I notice, and not in khakis, a possible trend I'd noticed previously on an airplane trip. (Does this mean Levi's are rising again, and The Gap is falling? It's something to check.)

Again, what I am looking for are *breaks in patterns.* I might hang out near the checkout lines for a while, and see what people are purchasing. The mere fact that there are a lot of people in Trader Joe's tells me many things. First, every dollar spent in a store like this on groceries is a dollar *not* spent in a store like Safeway. This represents permanently lost sales, which, if the inroads made by Trader Joe's are large enough, will have an impact on Safeway as a company. Second, the items sold at Trader Joe's represent discretionary dollars spent on food—not necessity dollars—so every dollar spent at Trader Joe's is also a dollar not spent on some other kind of consumer disposable, such as a CD or a movie ticket. The more money I see spent at Trader Joe's, the more I see meals not eaten in restaurants, sporting events not gone to, and the like.

When you are in your own neighborhood, doing the same thing that I'm doing now, you are witnessing the choices that consumers make. Whether you have a large amount of disposable income or a little, almost nobody has infinite resources. Every

139

choice made to buy one thing is a choice not to buy something else. It is not only a brand choice, but it is a *choice* choice, if you'll forgive the redundancy.

If you are an average American, you earn about $38,000 a year. After you pay for your taxes, your mortgage, your car payments and car insurance, and your clothes, you have about $1,000 a month in disposable income. Part of that goes for food, part of it for things like health insurance and homeowner's insurance, part for gas for your car, and the rest goes to whatever you want to spend it on. If you smoke a pack of cigarettes a day, for example, you are choosing to spend over $100 a month on cigarettes, or over $1,200 a year. The same thing is true if you go to Starbucks every day and buy yourself a *venti latte*. At the end of the year, you would have spent about 10 percent of your total disposable income on one single item.

If your household income is closer to $50,000 a year, you will probably have something close to $2,000 a month to spend on food, insurance, gas, and consumer disposables. That much money gives you some leeway when you are buying clothes, but not much, and if you have to make a big-ticket purchase, like a refrigerator or a stove, or a new television, it is going to put a real dent in your income. It's not until you get to a gross household income of about $75,000 that you have real purchasing power, because it is at that level that you begin to have enough money not only to spend, but to save and invest. At that point, you can make choices not only to satisfy present needs, but consider future needs, like vacations and owning a second home of your own, which will turn you into a consumer of an entirely different stripe.

The income group earning more than $100,000 per year is the fastest-growing group in the United States, having risen from 2 million households in 1990 to nearly 9 million in 2000. As the U.S. population becomes ever better educated, the number of people with large amounts of income and, hence, large amounts of disposable income, continues to rise in relation to the population. Every company wants a share of that rising income, so the number of new products will continue to grow. The number of new companies providing goods and services to that audience will also continue to grow.

What you are witnessing in the rise of the Internet is the rise of a channel that is meant to appeal to this rising affluent group. It is a group that has grown up with computers and cell phones, and thus sees nothing wrong and everything right with using both to do their buying and selling, if it can be made convenient enough. Right now, even though sales volumes are increasing, the Internet is still largely an experimental medium. Total retail sales are over $2 trillion, and the Internet accounts for only about $12 billion, which is less than 1 percent. But as people figure out the best ways to use the Internet, and it becomes more convenient to use, sales could rise sharply and rapidly. One of the reasons that technology stocks are so hot is that everybody is gambling that the combination of Internet and wireless technology will be the wave of the future, not only for upper-income people, but ultimately, for people with more average incomes as well. We'll come back to technology stocks in the next chapter, but for now, let's keep moving through the day.

I am heading for the doctor's office. I spend a lot of time playing basketball and softball when I'm not either in the office or on the road. I also run around a lot while I'm coaching my oldest son's basketball team, so sometimes my knees get a little stiff. At the doctor's I find his waiting room even more crowded than usual, and when it's my turn, I ask the nurse who is taking my blood pressure what's going on. She tells me about a new arthritis medication that has been advertised heavily in popular magazines. I live in an area where a lot of people wind up with arthritis-like symptoms. The daily grind of climbing San Francisco's steep hills, combined with the cold, humid weather is murder on your knees, even if you do keep in good shape. It's little wonder that so many people are here to see the doctor. Is this

141

a medical breakthrough and, if so, what are its implications? Take a look at the arthritis market. Which companies are making the drugs that are in the current generation, which will soon go off patent, and which companies are making the new drugs, which will replace them. In an aging marketplace, that's where the investment opportunities are.

Just before bed, I go through a couple of magazines. Are there articles about up-and-coming places to go, about new products? When I go through the newspaper, I look to see what kinds of jobs companies are hiring for. Employment advertising is one of the best indicators about how a company views itself. If it is hiring a lot of people, it probably expects sales to rise, or is about to make a large product push. If you see a company that advertises frequently for help, you ought to be looking into that company because you may be looking at a future investment.

When I watch television, I pay more attention to the commercials than to the programs because the commercials are about what people buy. But I also look at the programs, to get a general sense of how the programmers view the mood of the country. Are they showing more sitcoms or more dramas? It matters which.

The same goes for the movies. What's playing from week to week? In general, teens go to the movies twice as often as adults, so there are generally a lot of movies with teen themes. During the summer, when teens are not busy studying, the percentage of moviegoing teens rises even higher. What is playing at your local multiplex is a good indication of where the market for entertainment is going. If you see more serious dramas or independent films, it is an indication that consumers with disposable income want to be challenged intellectually and psychologically.

In a very real way, we live in a transactional society. Everything you see every day is the product of one company or another, and the more of something you see, the better that company is probably doing. It is doing well not only in terms of the products it actually sells, but it is also more successful in reaching out to you and persuading you to transact with it. Companies spend a substantial portion of their revenues persuading you to buy their products, and in getting those products into the channels where you buy. You have to be constantly looking at the channels themselves. When you go into general-merchandise stores—grocery stores, chain drugstores, warehouse stores, discount stores like Wal-Mart and Kmart, and department stores—be on the lookout for familiar products. In order to form a pattern, you need to see the same products in a lot of different places, which indicates that the company is making the greatest effort to get its products into the greatest number of channels.

Fewer channels brings you to one of two conclusions: Either the company is going to charge you more money for exclusivity, or the company is not doing a good job of getting its products across to the buying public. You can probably figure out which is which, though even some high-end companies like Tiffany and Cartier go to great lengths to get their merchandise into other high-end outlets—upscale department stores like Bloomingdale's.

In a transactional society, you are looking not only at what is bought, but also how and where it is sold. Be aware of the outlets through which a product is sold, lest you miss a significant channel. You might be calling up department-store buyers, only to find that most of what you are checking on is actually sold through discount stores. That's why the "where" is as important as the "what."

Let me give you an example. Until recently, large home appliances were sold either at appliance stores, Sears, Roebuck, or electronics discounters like Best Buy or Circuit City. Then Home Depot noticed that people were spending more money remodeling their homes, and began to sell appliances. I noticed this early on, and told my subscribers back in May 1999. Since then, Home Depot has risen from 40 to 70, a 75 percent gain. It has since fallen back a bit because of rising interest rates, which put a damper on home-equity loans used for improvements and expansion.

Years ago, Peter Lynch, who was then the manager of Fidelity's Magellan Fund, said that you could make a lot of money by investing in what people bought. The same strategy is still true, but you can't make any money if you don't observe those purchases, formulate some buying trends and patterns, and discover the companies taking advantage of these emerging patterns.

9

CONFIRM AND MEASURE

*Knowing the Critical Number
Every Industry Uses to Measure Itself*

Americans love to talk. They love to share and they love to teach, and they love to discuss just about anything with anyone who shows the slightest interest in what they have to say. If you don't believe me, hop on the Internet and go to any chatroom.

As a marketplace observer, you can legitimately ask people to confirm your observations, and they will likely give you more information than you might want. If you are in the supermarket and you see some new products, ask any of the employees, including the manager, how those products are doing, and they will tell you. If you see all those coffee stores, ask the owners and managers how they're doing, and they'll tell you.

In order to make your observations pay off, get into the habit of asking people to confirm your observations in a systematic way, and perhaps to provide a little interpretation of what they mean. It's not very efficient or useful to ask, "How's business?" Better to develop a theory, and then to ask pointed questions to test it. So if you notice that there are more varieties of Prego spaghetti sauce on the supermarket shelf than there used to be, and fewer varieties of Aunt Millie's, it's OK to ask the store manager, "Have sales of Aunt Millie's fallen off? Yes? How much? And I notice that there are more varieties of Prego. Are they bringing out a lot of new products?"

Now ask the same question in five or ten different supermarkets and compare the answers. Average the answers. How much do they differ? All of this put together will give you a pretty good picture of how spaghetti sauces are selling in your area.

You cannot ask one person about more than three issues at a time. Identify them and ask yourself how the answers will help you confirm or deny your theory. In asking questions, you should be open to an answer that sends you down an unexpected path. If you are asking your pharmacist about a new pain reliever that you think is going to be a big hit, and he tells you that he's sold a lot because the new eye-laser clinic in town just keeps ordering it, then you might want to follow up on the eye clinic and its implications. It's important to ask questions, but you have to develop an intellectual curiosity about the answers.

In this chapter, I am going to teach you what kinds of questions to ask, and how to make sense of the information you receive. The first part is the more difficult. The kind of questions you ask vary according to the industry you investigate, and to some of the larger macroeconomic issues of the day.

For example, let's say you are attempting to figure out a company's growth rate. You make a couple of calls, and your sources tell you that for the past quarter, the company has been growing at a 15 to 20 percent rate.

That sounds great, right? Well, maybe it does and maybe it doesn't. You want to know: "Is that rate of growth greater than that of competitors? Is it more or less than the quarter before? Is it more or less than the industry average? Is it more or less than companies in other sectors?" That's four questions right there, and each answer will have a different impact on your decision to buy or not buy the stock.

Start with the simplest question. If your company is growing its sales faster than its competitors, it is taking market share away from those competitors. Every dollar of sales my company makes is really worth two dollars because it is also a potential dollar denied to a competitor. So if the fast-food market is worth $1 billion per share point, a 1 percent shift in the market is worth $2 billion, assuming that the market doesn't grow—$1 billion that the winner gains, and $1 billion that its competitors lose.

But unless something catastrophic happens, chances are that each competitor will lose only a fraction of a share point before it begins to market its product heavily to the public. (That's one of the reasons that McDonald's and Burger King are among the largest advertisers in the United States. They can't afford to let customers migrate away in any significant number without alarm bells going off in their respective headquarters.) So, if your company is growing sales at a faster rate than competitors, that's a plus right off the bat.

But what if the entire industry is growing at a ferocious rate, like the cellular-phone industry in the 1990s. Ericsson, Nokia, Motorola, Qualcomm, and a number of Japanese companies literally then, could not build phones fast enough to satisfy global demand. (In fact, in May 2000, Motorola announced that it was going to outsource nearly $30 billion worth of manufacturing over to Flextronics, a contract electronics manufacturer.) The industry as a whole had a compound annual growth rate above 30 percent, and maintained that pace for several years. So if you are looking at a company whose growth rate is in the 15 to 20 percent range, you are looking at a company whose growth is about half the industry's average.

That's bad.

147

You also want to know if growth is more or less than the preceding quarter. Again, you have to know what 15 to 20 percent means, in relation to other data. If the sales of the company you are looking at were growing at a 5 percent rate for the last couple of quarters, 15 to 20 percent growth this quarter looks pretty good. But if your company had last-quarter sales growth of 50 percent, and three previous quarters of 30 percent, then a 15 to 20 percent growth rate means that sales are beginning to drop off. That's exactly what happened to Motorola in 1998, and the company was hammered by Wall Street, even though it was doing well.

Finally, is your industry doing as well as other industrial sectors? While it is true that there are superior companies in every sector, and that you can make money by investing in those companies, the sad truth is that you won't make as much money as if you had invested the same amount of money in a hotter sector. Wall Street loves growth, and it rewards the companies with the prospects of the highest growth with its highest P/E multiples. That's what explained the growth of Internet stocks; as long as Wall Street believed that the Internet and its companies had the potential to take over the world, it was willing to give them the money to do so, in the form of vastly inflated multiples. We'll come back to this lesson in Chapter 12, when we look at how professional traders make money on Wall Street, which is vastly different from the way that you and I make money.

Even before you get into growth rates, you want to ask a number of general and then specific questions. If you remember a chapter back, I talked about icebreaker questions, such as, "What is the general mood of shoppers?" They are not just small talk, they are questions designed to set the framework for the person you are interviewing. If you don't know that perspective, you will have a difficult time interpreting his or her answers, especially when you get into qualitative information. If the person you are speaking with has a generally negative view of his

148

or her industry, the answers you get are going to sound different from the answers of someone with a positive view.

Let's say that you are interested in the category of young women's clothing. If you talk to the managers of Wet Seal stores and Charming Shoppes, two national chains that market to teens and young women, and ask about customer confidence, and the retailer says that it is low, you have to evaluate the answer in light of what you know about consumer confidence from outside sources. You have to figure out why teenage girls are not buying as much as the marketplace in general.

In late 2001, consumer confidence as measured by The Conference Board and by the University of Michigan, two organizations that regularly analyze such things, was at or near an all-time high. Therefore, if a store manager told you that confidence among his or her customers is low, you have to ask, "What else is going on in town?"

Therefore, your next question should be, "Are there any special factors in your town that might account for that? Was there, for example, a big plant layoff, or a strike, or a large employer that moved out of town?" If the answer to any of those questions is yes, then everything that follows is out of the normal pattern and ought to be discarded at the outset. That particular interview subject is going to be of little help to you because any one of those events will ripple right through a town, causing all sorts of distortions in buying patterns.

So your first questions always have to be, "How are things in your town (city) (area)? Is customer confidence high or low? How do you think it compares to the national averages? Is there anything special going on in your town (city) (area) that would account for the difference?"

If you are doing research about an industrial company, those questions need to be rephrased. With few exceptions, industrial companies sell far beyond their local boundaries, so you should look for a read on factors affecting the industry.

Your first question should be, "How are things going in the industry? Is there anything special that's going on that is either bumping sales upward or holding them back?" You are likely to hear about raw-material problems or labor troubles. (Many traditional industries are heavily unionized, and contracts are set at the national level, so you need to know if there are any labor negotiations on the horizon. That is almost always a sell signal, at least for the short term.) If you had been asking these questions in the computer-hardware industry, for example, you would have turned up evidence of semiconductor shortages over the summer of 2000, months before companies like Dell Computer announced a third-quarter downturn in earnings.

The next thing you need to know is the metric (number) each industry uses to measure itself. Every industry has one. For example, in the airline, hotel, and car-rental businesses, it's the load factor. (In the hotel business, the load factor is called the "occupancy rate," but it's the same number.) Airline seats, hotel rooms, and car-rental opportunities are a time-perishable commodity. A seat not sold on a flight today is an opportunity lost forever.

Other industries that depend on time-sensitive selling are hospitals, which need to keep their beds full, and certain types of seasonal or perishable foods. In other industries, like semiconductors, and commodity products like wheat or corn, it is the overhang ratio, which simply means, "How much has been made versus how much has been sold?" In the semiconductor industry, it is called "the book-to-bill ratio," but it is really an overhang ratio. In oil, natural gas, agricultural commodities like soybeans and hog bellies—in fact, almost all of the industries where there are active futures markets—the overhang ratio is a key determinant of the profitability of one company over another.

For other industries, especially retailing, the key number is sales per square foot. It costs money, either as purchase, lease, or rental, to put up selling space, and those rates are calculated in dollars per square foot. In order for a store to be profitable, its sales per square foot have to be higher than the cost of the space, plus the cost of the merchandise in the store, and the cost of personnel and utilities, divided by square feet. If the average store is 10,000 square feet, and the average rental is $52 per square foot per year, the store must bring in a minimum of $10,000 per week just to cover the use of the space. If the store then pays $3,000 per week in salaries, and $500 a week for utilities (phone and electricity), plus the amortization of the fixtures (say another $1,000) per week, the store has to bring in nearly $15,000 per week just to cover its overhead. If it sells goods at a 100 percent markup over wholesale, the store needs to sell more than $1.5 million worth of merchandise per year just to break even, or nearly $4,200 a day, or $2.87 per square foot per week.

When you are asking about sales per square foot, be sure that whoever you are talking with tells you the unit of time (per week, per day, per month, per quarter).

Retail analysts will often do what they call "comps," or same-store comparables. One of the ways to tell the health of a company is to see what the sales per square foot are after a year, and compare it to both the company's average, and to sales for the store when it first opened. Many retailers make it appear that they are growing by constantly opening new stores. The novelty of a store appearing with new merchandise, or a new concept, will often give a company the glow of health, while same-store sales, or comps, are falling. That's exactly what happened with Boston Market, and it is now happening with McDonald's as well. Given the general fickleness of the U.S. buying public, it is very difficult to sustain any retailing concept over time.

Once you have determined what the appropriate key number is, direct your efforts to putting it within a comparative framework. Numbers mean nothing unless they are compared to other numbers, so you need to ask questions like, "How does your number compare to the industry average? Is the industry moving up or down this year? What are the factors driving the changes? Are you buying or selling more or less than at the same time last year?"

Companies often publish this data in their annual reports, but you have to hunt for it. McDonald's annual report, for example, tells you how many stores it has, how many new stores, and what the sales per year are. You can derive the sales per store per year as well as the sales per new store from these numbers. You don't need sales per square foot. You will find, indeed, that sales at new stores are higher than the average sale. If you really want to dig deeper, get five years of annual reports and make a table. You will see that there has been a slow, but persistent decline of new store sales as well. That means that Americans are no longer as facinated with McDonald's concept, which is why the stock has been an underperformer for some time.

The best way to approach the problem is to write down a series of no more than ten questions. One or two should be scene setters, and the rest should be designed to give you information that is both specific and within the bounds of what people are allowed to tell you.

Once you have written down your questions, print them out on a sheet of paper and make enough copies to do multiple interviews. These sheets should be labeled with the name of your source and his or her phone and fax number, as well as an E-mail address if you can get one. Then you can ask additional questions if you need to follow up, and share information with all of the people you asked, and other members of your group, if you have one. Now begin making your phone calls. Remember to be persistent, and to be accurate in writing down what you are told.

Ultimately, you are looking always for percentage increases or decreases in sales or profits, which is very specific information. When framing percentage questions, it helps to keep percentages within fairly narrow ranges. For example, if you are researching the candy industry, ask a store candy buyer if he or she is buying 5 percent more from a manufacturer than in the previous quarter, instead of asking how much. If the buyer says more than 5 percent, ask if it is more than a 10 percent increase. If he or she says yes, keep going until you get a no answer. To make recording percentages simpler, make a set of boxes on your sheet that rise in 5 percent increments, so you can check off the appropriate box. When you hear the word "no," or "it isn't that high," put an X in the last box, so you know that you have reached the end of that question.

Before you begin your interviews, make sure that the people you are calling represent a broad mix of information related to your product. When you are first trolling for information sources, don't be afraid to ask a potential source how much of a market he or she controls. If you have someone who buys for one store, that's not much of a source; but if you have someone who buys for a hundred-store chain, that person is a coveted buyer not only for companies seeking to sell their wares, but for you as well. Seek to get as many "power" sources of this kind as possible, and cultivate them well. They will make your job a lot easier.

After you have done at least ten interviews, it is time to score them. You want to add up the percentage ranges that each source has given you, and get an average percentage. But first you have to weight your percentages. Someone who buys for 100 stores is worth a lot more than someone who buys for only one store, unless the one store is so large and the 100 so small that it affects results. In order to weight your percentages properly, you need a little more information. You need a multiplier.

Let's go all the way back to Chapter 2, where we looked at P&G, Colgate Palmolive, Clorox, and Johnson & Johnson. Procter & Gamble's sales are about twice as large as J&J's, about four times larger than Colgate's, and about sixteen times as large as Clorox. So when a buyer from a drugstore chain tells you that he is increasing his sales of Clorox products by 10 percent, it means a lot to Clorox; but in the context of competition,

it means relatively little to P&G. Since you have already done
your industry and company calculations, you will know what a
dollar of sales is worth to each company in your category. If the
same buyer told you that his purchases of P&G products were
up only 5 percent, the dollar value would be worth sixteen times
as much as a comparable rise in Clorox products. That's the
kind of multiplier we're talking about.

Multipliers are the steep hill of competition, why it is so
difficult for smaller companies to become larger companies.
Take the example of Clorox and P&G. If P&G sales did not
grow at all, and Clorox sales grew at 15 percent a year, it
would take Clorox more than twenty years to catch up to
P&G's current sales rate. If P&G grew by only 5 percent a year
during that time, it would take Clorox nearly forty years to
overtake Procter & Gamble. So while percentage increases are
important in the short run, it is important to evaluate them
and calculate their impact in the long run.

Back to information averaging. Let us say that your panel of
ten buyers answered the question, "What does the percentage in
P&G products purchased by you look like?" The answers might
look like this:

	Number of Stores	Total Store Sales (in billions)	Percent Increase/ Decrease	Weight
Buyer A	100	$1.00	+5	1.3
Buyer B	250	2.20	+3	3.3
Buyer C	60	.75	+7	0.8
Buyer D	25	.10	−10	0.3
Buyer E	150	1.50	−3	2.0
Buyer F	10	.05	+12	0.2
Buyer G	25	.12	−5	0.3
Buyer H	25	.15	+5	0.3
Buyer I	80	.75	+3	1.1
Buyer J	30	.75	+12	0.4

If you simply averaged the numbers without using a multiplier, you'd come up with about an average 3 percent gain for all ten buyers. But if you do a little more arithmetic, you'll see that there are other valuable numbers on the page. The average number of stores is 75 stores per buyer. Each buyer is therefore weighted by what multiple of 75 he or she represents (see Weight above). When those weights are multiplied times the percentage increase, they give an overall percentage change of less than 2 percent, which is a very modest increase, indeed, in percentage terms, but a healthy increase for P&G relative to its competitors, since just those 2 percentage points are worth $1 billion in sales.

In order to come up with meaningful comparisons, it isn't enough to just check on P&G. You have to ask the percentage gain or lost questions of all the competitors, until you have a set of columns of numbers that will tell you whether the market as a whole is growing, or whether one competitor is growing at the expense of its rivals, and whether any of that growth is in excess or below the rate of the economy as a whole.

Now you have enough information to make the beginning of a marketplace-check-based investment decision.

You could probably stop here, but you'll want to check some assumptions. So, if you see that one of the competitors in a category is growing at a faster rate, the logical question to ask is, "How are they doing it?" Companies have several ways to boost sales. One is to manufacture a better product, or to offer a "new, improved" version of their product, or to attempt to build brand identity through advertising. Such attempts are indirect inducements to consumers, and, when they work, they can boost a company's bottom line quite well.

Other forms of inducement include couponing, sampling, manufacturer's rebates, and store promotions. All of these are attempts to boost short-term sales artificially by providing an artificial discount to a product's price to give it a temporary price advantage over the competition.

This form of promotion is considered unhealthy. It is a "rob Peter to pay Paul" mentality. People consume products at a fairly steady rate once their households are established. You don't use extra soap just because it suddenly goes on sale, do you? Or use extra razor blades? Of course you don't.

When packaged goods go on sale or you find a juicy coupon offer in your Sunday newspaper that compels you to buy extra, you are doing what is known as "forward buying." You are buying today what you are going to use tomorrow, and that means that you are *not* going to buy tomorrow. Manufacturers with many brands, like Sara Lee, which has more than 150 brands, or Unilever, which has several hundred, take consumers' forward buying into account by doing "rolling promotions": couponing a different set of brands each month in hopes of avoiding the forward-buying problem.

However, at a certain point, your shelves are loaded with merchandise that you are not consuming. This was not much of a problem all through the 1970s and 1980s, when coupon redemption rates were high, and inflation made buying today cheaper than waiting for tomorrow. But low inflation, falling coupon-redemption rates—they are now below 2 percent and are dropping about 0.1 percent per year—and a trend toward smaller houses as baby boomers become empty nesters is emptying out the personal hoards of people who stockpiled goods that were on sale. That makes it more difficult for companies that use coupons to drive sales to record permanent sales gains.

Therefore, one of your follow-up questions to merchants or buyers should be, Are any of the companies we spoke about earlier doing heavy coupon or store promotion? (A store promotion is just like couponing, except that the consumer doesn't see the tangible evidence of the promotion. The savings are passed through to the consumer by the store, in return for the store's stocking more of a given product. Whenever you see ads where a store brags about its huge "buying power" to provide discounts to customers, it's a sure sign that they have store promotion deals with manufacturers.)

Why do manufacturers risk future sales on such promotions? First, they are driven by a constant need to make their numbers by Wall Street analysts who will downgrade any company that does not produce consistent growth. Second, managers inside a company are promoted on the basis of meeting or exceeding their own numbers; so when a manager is coming up for promotion or review, he or she has a natural tendency to want to goose the numbers to look better to the bosses.

Finally, it's all about store shelf space. It's one thing to put more products on the shelves, but it is quite another to get consumers to buy. Manufacturers often trade promotions of existing popular products for future shelf space for new products they plan to introduce. Store owners always want to go with the manufacturers whose products sell the most, so they allocate shelf space on the basis of a combination of unit sales and unit profitability. Before they will give over a foot of shelf space to a new product from an established manufacturer, they have to be convinced that there will be more sales per foot.

Therefore, another one of your follow-up questions needs to be, "Do you know if Company X is planning any major new products or line extensions in your store over the next three months?"

The answer will tell you two things: First, whether the store has been helping the manufacturer to temporarily drive sales at the expense of its competition. Second, it will give you a distant early warning about the arrival of a new product or category on the store shelves, which gives you another bit of information to consider: whether the new product is likely to boost or hurt sales of the company you are following. If it is a product that already has many competitors, the company is going to have to spend a lot of money promoting it to see any result. If it is a product that has relatively little competition, the company may get a good-sized rise in sales for its efforts.

As you can see, you can develop quite a lot of information about companies just by asking questions. With even minimal responses, you can draw some interesting conclusions. Now let's take some of that information into the real world. This will be an exercise in information correlation.

Do you remember in the previous chapter, in my visit to Safeway, I noted that organic and natural foods have begun to appear on the same shelves as other foods, and are no longer segregated by themselves? This indicates that they are now normal category players, and are therefore worthy of consideration as legitimate competitors with more established companies.

A good example of this trend is the announcement at the end of May 2000, that Hain Food Group had decided to buy Celestial Seasonings, a maker of specialty teas. Hain is a rapidly growing company that specializes in natural and organic foods. Together, the two companies have sales of only about $430 million, a drop in the bucket compared to Unilever's more than $23 billion in sales.

Yet you know that something is afoot, because both Hain and Celestial Seasonings prices rose on news of the merger, while the price of Unilever dropped when it announced plans to buy Best-foods, the maker of such brands as Skippy Peanut Butter and Thomas' English Muffins, at almost the same time.

Why does Wall Street approve of one deal and not the other? Think about it. If "healthy" and organic foods are becoming part of the mainstream, Hain's sales will probably rise faster than the food category as a whole, and it will be able to command more total shelf space for its products by adding those of Celestial Seasonings. Meanwhile, Wall Street's food analysts feel that Unilever already has more brands on its plate than it can reasonably manage. Moreover, if Hain continues to grow, it may be acquired at a hefty premium sometime in the future, because it will have a large share of a growing category. So if you are checking in the food category, Hain Celestial, as the new company is called, probably becomes a new stock to watch.

These are all things that you need to be thinking about as you formulate your questions. What is going on in the larger marketplace that might have an impact on what I am researching? Are there new players just under the radar who might become important? At Off The Record Research, we follow a couple of hundred companies out of *tens* of thousands. These represent the largest holdings of the largest funds. These are the companies that our clients buy and sell, and so they need the right information on these companies at the right time. But we are always keeping our eyes open for the appearance of new competitors, and attempting to figure out what their appearance means. For example, in the Salty Snack category, we obviously watch Frito-Lay (Pepsico). It completely dominates the market as few companies ever have. But we also watch Pringle's (Procter & Gamble) to see how they are faring. Besides the producers of chips, we look at very closely related emerging products. When we report on Salty Snacks, we make sure we ask about both nutritional bars and meat jerky to see whether they are making any inroads in the category.

Marketplace checks are the fastest way to uncover potential new competitors. You have to learn how to view the supermarket, the drugstore, and the discount store as arenas for competition, but supermarkets are the Super Bowl, precisely because they carry so many different products and categories in such a limited amount of space. The collective decisions of every consumer determines what is kept on the shelves and what goes, and manufacturers are willing to spend billions of dollars on advertising and promotion to influence your choice. This is the stuff of high drama because it translates directly into the prices people are willing to pay for the shares of companies, into careers made and broken, and into multibillion-dollar merger and acquisition deals. When you purchase a can of soup or a bar of soap, you are stepping onto a huge stage and participating in an ongoing play that can be high theater or low camp. When manufacturers make their biggest mistakes, such as when Coca-Cola changed its formula, or Ford introduced the Edsel, it might not cripple a company, but it can change its fortunes for years, recast the boardroom, and spell disaster for shareholders and money managers alike. By deciding to become a marketplace checker, you not only give yourself a front-row seat on the action, you have the chance to become a part of the action yourself.

I won't kid you. Just as your individual purchasing decisions mean nothing, your individual stock-buying decisions mean almost nothing. You are buying a couple of hundred shares while large institutions are buying and selling tens of thousands of shares. But if enough people who read this book decide to become active marketplace checkers, the information flow in the marketplace begins to change—first just a tiny amount, and then at a much faster rate.

Forming teams and exchanging information with and among team members increases your leverage because collectively, you might buy or sell as many shares as an institution. If you are buying or selling against a trend and volume suddenly begins to rise, Wall Street takes notice. Some bright technical analyst—the kind that follows the up and down movements of stocks in an attempt to discern patterns—will notice your collective movement and begin to ask questions. He or she won't call you, but will call a fellow analyst who follows the industry from a different perspective. If that analyst is smart, he or she will then begin to do exactly the same kind of digging that you have already done.

If you've come to the right conclusions, so will the analyst. And when that happens, the analyst's recommendation on the company is likely to change. And then Wall Street takes notice. With a little work on your part and many more like you, you will have done what you thought was impossible: moved a stock in your favor.

10

SEARCHING FOR ADDITIONAL INFORMATION

By doing a good job with your marketplace checks, you will be building up a steadily increasing number of people to whom you can turn for information. But what happens when the people you are talking to give you information that is contradictory, or adds up to nothing? This is not as uncommon as it might seem. Often, when a marketplace is functioning normally, nothing much is going on. In the previous chapter, I likened competition in the marketplace to passionate drama, but it is often more like trench warfare, with competitors moving back and forth across the same territory over and over again. Can you make money in such an environment? Should you bother?

The answer to both questions is yes. On-line trading has greatly lowered the transaction cost of buying and selling, so you don't have to pay nearly as big a penalty for moving in and out of stocks. I am not talking about becoming a day trader, but rather, an increasingly periodic trader. If you track a group of stocks every month, you will get to know a lot more about your companies than many professional investors.

163

Each time you find a discrepancy between what you know and what the market knows, that represents an opportunity to trade. If, for example, your monthly research tells you that one competitor is on track to post even modest gains against an industry group, you can buy put options (the potential winner) or sell short (the potential losers), if you are confident that the news on which you are buying and selling will turn up in the marketplace before the end of the quarter. During the 1980s, this so-called "pairs" strategy, of finding two comparable companies in the same industry, and then buying one while shorting the other, produced fortunes for several traders. The pairs trading of the 1980s died out when it became clear that most of the trades were by professional traders feeding off each other's buy and sell decisions, and not because of any real information affecting the price of the shares.

You do not have to actually buy or sell stocks to engage in a pairs-trading system. If you have a computer, you can make hypothetical buy and sell trades on a spreadsheet and keep track of the results, until you are confident either that what you are doing has some merit, or that the information on which you are basing your decisions is sound. One of the most important things to know about a marketplace-check-based investing system is that it is not foolproof. One of the reasons that we do so much research at OTR is that the more we do, the greater the confidence we have in our results. But remember: We are sampling only a fraction of a universe of buyers, so that our samples are never going to be 100 percent reliable. Instead, we operate on the basis of a confidence level.

In statistics, a confidence level is a relationship between the size and quality of a sample and the whole that it represents. For example, if the total universe of people I need to talk to is 100, and I speak with all 100 of them, and I assume that all of these people tell me the truth, I am 100 percent confident that the answers I have come up with are accurate. If I only speak to

164

10 people, my confidence level might drop as low as 10 percent, or be as high as 90 percent. It will all depend upon who those 10 people are. If they are highly representative of the group, then my confidence in their answers will be high. The less representative of the group they are, the lower my confidence level is going to be.

You must know something about the group before you can begin to construct your sample. Let's say the industry you are covering is cellular phones. If you call their industry association, you will be able to find out how many members it has and how many stores and sales outlets they represent. The number of stores and sales outlets is the size of your sample. Let's say it is 100,000. A friendly chat with the representative of the industry association, or someone from the Consumer Electronics Industry Association, might tell you that the top 100 vendors account for 35 percent of sales, through their approximately 10,000 stores.

In doing your research, it is obvious that the greater the number of people you can question who are among those top 100 vendors, or buy for them, the greater the confidence your answers will have. Here's why: Every dollar you spend in one store is a dollar you are not spending in another. If the top 100 vendors account for 35 percent of sales, it means that they account for those sales through only 10 percent of the stores. The other 90 percent of stores account for only 65 percent of sales. If you turn both of those relationships into fractions, you get the following: 35/10 versus 65/90, or a ratio which simplifies to 1:0.206. In other words, that means that each unit of sales in one of the top 100 vendors is worth nearly five times as much as a unit of sales in a vendor below the top 100.

Such weightings are the heart and soul of putting together your list and giving your results the degree of confidence you need for making a decision on a stock.

Often, the weighting of units is enough to tip the scales. But sometimes, you have to construct "dollar-weighted" averages. In many product categories, there are wide disparities in the prices of goods, so that a store could conceivably have a low unit volume but have a dollar volume that is just as high as a store that sold more units because it sells more expensive merchandise. For example, Calvin Klein sells his jeans for more than $50 a pair, while you can buy a good pair of Arizona store brand jeans at JCPenney for about $20. For the Penney's jeans buyer to have the same clout as the buyer for the much smaller Dillard's department store chain, which sells Calvin Klein jeans, the Penney's buyer has to sell 2.5 pairs of jeans for every pair that Dillard's sells, just to keep even.

This leads to a whole new level of questions, those relating to price. One of the things that you are going to be interested in, especially with branded goods, is the price premium that they are able to command in the marketplace. There is not much difference between a pair of jeans made by Calvin Klein and one made by Penney's, but people are willing to pay a 150 percent or more price premium for the jeans with the Calvin Klein label. That premium is the real value of a company like Calvin Klein—not the quality of the clothes it sells, no matter how good that quality is.

In fact, according to several studies done over the years, brand value, as reflected in price premiums, makes up as much as 90 percent of the actual value of a company, as opposed to the "book" value, which is what the physical plant and machinery are worth. The difference between book value, which is often just a fraction of share value, and brand value is called "goodwill" on a company's balance sheet. That goodwill is of critical importance to you as a marketplace checker. When you go out into the marketplace and look at what people are buying, you are really looking at what people think of the brands they are consuming and, hence, what the goodwill of a company is worth.

A company's brands are its most important assets. People used to think that technology was important; but in the 1970s and the 1980s, the Japanese proved that technology alone, in the absence of constant innovation, was not worth very much. Japanese engineers found that they could buy licenses to American technology, and then design products that got around the wall of patents that protected the parts of technology that were not for sale. The Japanese used a simple principle: What one person knows, another person can learn. This insight of the Japanese almost brought Xerox to its knees during the 1980s, and it killed off much of the American consumer-electronics industry. It wasn't until companies began investing in the value of their brands, by building stronger relationships with their customers in the late 1980s and early 1990s, that the American economy began to recover, and then grow. Today, companies do everything they can to cultivate their brands, and to keep their customers happy.

In this environment, consumers can become very demanding, so brands have to work very hard. They not only have to be well maintained and well known, but they also need to be relevant to customers. Relevance is extremely important. You may know the Rolls-Royce brand name but, unless you are extremely rich, it isn't relevant to you. You aren't going to own a Rolls, so you don't care whether its brand attributes meet your needs. But Rolls-Royce has to care very much about the people who can afford to buy its product, and who might. Those potential customers are the subject of extensive research.

Brand maintenance is also important for products as mundane as salad dressing and toilet paper. Companies are constantly looking to invest their brands with enough relevance to a large enough pool of potential customers so that their brands provide a return that is a very large multiple of their investment in advertising and couponing. That is good news for you as a marketplace checker, especially with well-known consumer brands.

Advertising is one of those markers that lets you know what is going on with a product or category. If you pay attention to the advertising on television, radio, and in print, and you suddenly see a blitz of ads for a product, you know that something is going on at the company that makes the product. Somebody has decided that either the margins on the product have fallen below a certain level, or that the product has suddenly become very profitable, because the machinery that makes it has been fully amortized. In either case, whether for positive or negative reasons, the company feels the need to invest in this particular brand. If you begin to ask "why" questions of your panels, you will probably find out some interesting things about the company. For example: "I've noticed that Gillette is suddenly doing heavy promotion on White Rain shampoo. That's an old brand from the 1950s. Are they bringing it back? Is it being sold as a premium brand or as a bargain brand? How are the comparable sales in that category going?"

The answers to these questions tell you about the direction in which the marketplace is moving. If White Rain, which is a discount brand, is selling well, what does that mean? It may be taking share away from other bargain brands, in which case it is a zero-sum game. Or it may be taking share away from premium brands, in which case those brands are losing relevance with consumers.

Here's another example. Ten years ago—even five years ago—consumers were interested in fat-free foods. Companies like Nabisco Group Holdings were developing new brands like Snackwells to cash in on the trend, and those new brands, because they were relevant to consumer needs, sold extremely well.

But within the past few years, people have suddenly grown tired of fat-free foods. They want the richer taste that butterfat imparts. So brands like Snackwells are now languishing. Snackwells' ads have disappeared from television, and the amount of shelf space for the products has shrunk faster than a dieter's waistline. Paying attention to advertising does not only mean looking at TV ads and listening to the radio. One of the best ways to know what is going on in a company or an industry is to read the help-wanted ads, especially in *The Sunday New York Times* or *The Sunday Washington Post,* and in *The Wall Street Journal's National Business Employment Weekly.*

The most important ads to look at are the large display ads for professional and managerial help. In order for a company to grow, it has to hire key people *before* a new product or subsidiary is launched. It has to get those people in place in order to get the product made, distributed, marketed, and advertised. Help-wanted advertising is a six-month look-ahead into a company's future. Generally, it takes that long from the time a new team is hired until a product is launched or a new initiative bears fruit.

When you notice a company hiring a lot of people, determine whether this is a company or industry you should follow. What does the new hiring represent? Is it turmoil in management? If so, that says something negative about a company's future. Is it for a new product or new service or subsidiary? That might say something positive, as well as tell you that the competitive landscape of an industry might be about to change. Why is the company hiring, and where is the money coming from?

Go back to the balance sheet and look at the company's cash reserves. Right after a new round of hiring is announced, if the reserves are going down, the company is investing hard-won money from the past in the future. If, on the other hand, the company is able to invest out of current cash flow, that's much better, because the reserves give it a cushion if the new product fails to meet expectations. Your job as a marketplace checker is to find out what it all means.

Find out whether or not the sales of the items you are tracking are seasonal. Many retailers lose money for three quarters and then more than make up their losses during the Christmas selling season. In some industries, especially giftware, more than two-thirds of all sales take place in the month between Thanksgiving and Christmas, so it pays to listen to buyers and retailers alike if you are dealing with seasonal trends.

Not all seasonal buying revolves around Christmas. Snowblowers and other winter merchandise sell in the late fall and early winter. A company like Toro can be felled by a mild winter, which is why it branched off into lawn mowers, to add an additional selling season. But that doesn't always work, either. A drought or a wet spell can cut down on the amount of lawn mowing and, as more competitors like Honda have entered the field, the lawn-mower business has become relatively less attractive. Spring and summer are also big for items like patio furniture, barbecue equipment, and nursery supplies. Early fall and early spring are big clothes-selling seasons—warm-weather clothes for spring and summer and back-to-school clothes are the reason—and even gasoline consumption is seasonal. Many more people drive during their summer vacations, and go longer distances. So you need to pay attention to *when* people are buying things as well as *if* they are buying them. Make year-over-year comparisons. Is this winter season better or worse than last winter? Did consumers buy more or less? *These* are the questions you have to ask.

In order to develop confidence in the answers that you receive, it is not enough to achieve some statistical consistency. You can have full agreement from all of the buyers or retailers, but if your observations are out of sync with what you are being told, you have to press forward and ask "why" questions. These are the hardest questions to answer because they are "bounce-back" questions. A bounce-back question is one where the person being questioned turns the tables and asks you, "Well, why do you think you are observing what you say you are seeing?"

You now have to account for your own observations and, if you are new to marketplace checking, that's going to be difficult. Often, you are observing a skewed sample. Let's say, for example, that you notice five girls walking around in a shopping center, and they are all wearing black dresses. Is that really a trend, or is it just five girls walking around in black dresses. You reflect on what you've noticed, and get on the phone and call other people. In conversation, ask them if they've noticed a lot of teenaged girls walking around in black dresses.

Right away, you have committed one of the cardinal sins of observation. You have biased the observer. All of the people you've called are now going to go to their own local malls, or hang around near schools, and begin counting girls in black dresses.

Guess what? They are going to see some—probably a number sufficient for you all to believe that you are catching the edge of the next great fashion trend. Many years ago, physicist Werner Heisenberg noticed this tendency for observers to bias what they see when he was studying the motion of the electron. He called this the "Uncertainty Principle." What applies to the motion of spinning electrons also applies to the observations that marketplace checkers make.

Your job as team leader is not only to make observations, but also to control the process of questioning. If you notice what you think is a trend, make sure that you and your team are asking the right questions. So, if you are interviewing a fashion buyer or a fashion editor, your questions need to be in stages: "Have you noticed any significant trends or changes in the kinds of dresses teenaged girls are purchasing?" Or, "I've noticed lately that there seem to be a lot of girls wearing little black dresses. Do you notice the same thing? Is this a trend or is it just something that a few girls are wearing?" In other words, you have to be a little tentative in your rush to form hypotheses from your observations. You can't just see and assume.

Newly minted marketplace checkers tend to place the new above the old. As we'll see in the next chapter, this can easily send you off in the wrong direction. Americans are fascinated with new things, with new clothes, with new consumer goods.

Many people are up on the latest trends and fads, and can tell you in an instant if they are looking at the latest model of CD player or last year's model.

But being focused entirely on the new is a trap. Companies often cannot sell all of the merchandise they make, so they have to sell it beyond their regular sales channels, often at a higher profit than their newest items. The newest stuff a company makes costs the most money to make because usually the company has invested in new tooling and new equipment to make it. However, when a company gets a long production run, its cost-per-item-manufactured goes down, often way down. The company can then sell an item like a CD player through a discount channel, and still make a handsome profit. If you see a lot of people walking around with what appears to be last year's model, you might well conclude that the company's current sales are weak. And you might well be wrong.

To develop real confidence in the marketplace, you also need to know not only which channels sell the most, but how many different channels a company uses. Does a company sell at outlets, through company stores? Companies such as leather goods and shoe maker Etienne Aigner, for example, sell a lot of merchandise through company stores and depend on those sales as much as from department stores. Because these channels are different, the company develops different lines for each channel.

But if you don't know this, you will jump to the wrong conclusion. You will think that the merchandise you see in a company store is discounted or out-of-fashion merchandise, especially if the company store is located in an outlet mall. Most people have it fixed in their heads that the latest and best merchandise is in the department stores, that discount stores get the next best, and that outlets get the seconds, overruns, and discontinued merchandise. If you think that way, you will be missing out on the opportunity to find out what is actually going on in the marketplace.

Learn the selling structure of the company that you are following. What are its regular channels of distribution, and how much merchandise is sold, through each channel. If you can learn to figure out the profit margins of each channel, so much the better, but you don't really need to. You are simply attempting to get comparative numbers. You want to know if people are buying more through one channel or another than they were in the same quarter last year, and if they are buying more than in the quarter before.

The use of the Internet as an alternative distribution channel also has to be considered. For instance, let's assume you are tracking car rentals. You may be doing this for several reasons. First you may be following Hertz, Avis, Dollar, Thrifty, or one of the other rental companies. If you are, you need to know how much of the companies' revenues and income derive from retail car rentals. Alternatively, you may be interested in tourism in a certain area, and are looking at car rentals as an indicator of that market.

Whatever the reason, you need to be aware of changes in the distribution channel. Let's say that you call large travel agents, or people who run the travel departments of large companies, and you find that bookings for rental cars are down 5 percent year to year. Ordinarily, this would be considered a negative input. But what if people are now starting to book their own reservations over the Internet. If Internet bookings represent 5 percent of rentals, this is not very important. But what if they represent 25 percent of bookings, and they are up 18 percent year to year. Then you need to somehow factor in the bookings through this new distribution channel. All of this is legitimate grist for your information mill.

There is one more inconsistency of data to discuss before we continue. Many times, when we are collecting information at OTR, we find that there is no seeming pattern in the data. When that happens, we ask ourselves, "Where is the data coming from?" Data have a different meaning depending on what part of the country it comes from. If you get information from the coasts—especially from California and New York and their sub-urbs—it means something different than if you get it from Iowa. Generally, trends begin on the coasts and work their way inland. That's true whether the trends originate in the tony boutiques of Madison Avenue and Rodeo Drive, or in Harlem or Watts. Rich or poor, people tend to copy what's in the biggest cities, and that means New York and Los Angeles.

That does not mean that when you observe something in New York or L.A., you are automatically going to see it in Dubuque or St. Louis in six months or a year. Many trends are a little too hip to migrate much beyond the big city, and some-times there are factors that can impede the flow of a trend. Take sushi. You've been able to get good sushi in New York and L.A. for nearly thirty years, but you'd be hard-pressed to find it in most inland cities. It's not because people in small inland towns don't like raw fish over rice, it's because there are just not many Japanese or Korean sushi chefs migrating to these places. Nor are there good sources of supply for raw ocean fish, like tuna and mackerel.

The geographic nature of data is not just related to fads. It exists in basics such as clothing and food. Back in April 1999, we told our clients about a company called Pacific Sunwear of California, whose clothing sales were surging. After our report, the stock began to surge, too, rising 56 percent in a single year. If you've been hit with the second deep snowfall of the winter, you may find all the snowblowers in town are out of stock. This is undoubtedly good for the Toro Company, but unless the snows are coming down in a wide area, it's not going to mean much. You need to determine how wide spread the heavy winter is. Is it just in upstate New York, or has it spread across a wider area, and into marginal places? Locations which usually don't see much snowfall are likely to be first-time buyers. Also are the snows coming in early November (where people might be ready to invest for a long winter) or in late March, when many will just wait it out? Learn to take geography into account when you spot what looks to be a promising trend.

Therefore, when you are in the midst of observing, you must ask yourself, "From what vantage point am I observing, and how does that skew my data?" This is another variant on Heisenberg's Uncertainty Principle, and it is something that you have to carry around in your head as you are doing your checking. In an early chapter, I said that you need to strive for geographic diversity in your team and on your panels. This geographic diversity will help you confirm whether what you are seeing is worthy of follow-up. Generally, if you make an observation in the middle of the country, you have to make the same observation on the coasts before you can consider it to be trendworthy. That sounds as if I have a bias against the heartland of America, but I don't.

Also, while the rule is generally true, sometimes it is not true in a big way. For decades, New York was the leading force in retailing innovation. Christmas as we know it, as a huge holiday of gift giving, was essentially invented by New York department stores and catalog merchants in the late nineteenth century. New York's boutiques and fashion industry are still in the avant garde of men's and women's clothing trends.

But in many other areas, New York is no longer an innovator. Many of the largest and most successful retailing trends have started outside of New York, in the heartland, and worked their way outward across the country. Wal-Mart began in tiny Bentonville, Arkansas. Home Depot began in Atlanta. Delivered pizza, like Domino's and Papa John's, originated in Michigan. Ray Kroc discovered the McDonald brothers in rural California, and then moved his hamburger franchising company to Illinois. Many of the most successful modern retailing chains have started in the heartland and have ignored New York altogether, not even bothering to open stores there until very late in the game, because of New York's very high real-estate costs. So while trends tend to originate on the coasts, there is nothing to presuppose that the Next Big Thing will not start right in your own hometown. That's why marketplace checking is both interesting and important.

All of this can be a little bit daunting. If you are not used to the processes of marketplace checking—noticing, collecting, and analyzing information that is all around you—you may begin to think that this process is just way too complicated for what you are going to get out of it. I can only encourage you to try marketplace checking, on the grounds that if you don't do it, you are never going to have the chance to make yourself a better, smarter investor. Moreover, as knowledge is power, learning how to observe and analyze will make you better at whatever you decide to do with your life, even if it is not investing.

11

SEPARATING WINNERS FROM LOSERS

Making Your Marketplace Checks Pay

Once you have asked your questions, gathered your data, and come to your conclusion, you need to apply three more tests to determine if this is information that is relevant to making an investment decision.

1. Is it a major investment issue? You might discover that a new pet food for cats is becoming extremely popular. You then discover that the company which makes the cat food gets only 15 percent of its revenues from cat food and 85 percent from dog food. Even worse, the company is a division of a large agribusiness company. The entire division contributes less than 5 percent of the parent company's net income.

In this example, you have done everything right, and you have discovered something unusual. But it is not going to have any meaningful impact on the parent company, so you can't derive a useful investment decision from your discovery.

This is not always true. If you are intellectually curious, you should still look at the company's annual report and see if other divisions are coming out with new products. If they are, find out how some of them are doing. If you get enough positive reports on enough new products, then you do have a positive investment decision.

Moreover, while the rising sales of the cat food made by the company you are following may have no impact on that company, they do have an impact on the industry as a whole. Is there a competitor who derives more revenue and profit from the sale of cat food? Is it publicly traded? Does its stock price reflect the fact that a competitor is doing much better? If the stock price doesn't reflect this news, then you can short the stock profitably or if you own it, sell before the news gets out.

Whether or not your research is investment-worthy is a big part of what makes this book important. If you don't do the research, you'll never know if a bit of information has relevance, and you will remain in the world of rumors. If you are diligent about observing and analyzing, you will know in a way that investors around you won't. This is the difference between originated wisdom and received wisdom. Most people, and most of life, rely on received wisdom. You do things because people tell you that what you are doing is the right way to proceed. Most of what you learn in school, most of what you learn from your parents, most of what you learn on the job is received wisdom, passed along and down from person to person. Received wisdom is the collective knowledge of society, and it is useful for maintaining the status quo.

But investing is not about the status quo at all. It is about change, and when the landscape is changing and you are receiving new information, you have to either fit it against the received wisdom of the past, or attempt to originate some wisdom of your own. Admittedly, very few people are original thinkers, but you're not creating Newton's Law of Gravity.

When you are attempting to ascertain relevance, you are forced to look at the big picture, and to use your imagination.

You are forced to draw inferences, the suggestions of linkages between Fact A and Investment Q. A couple of chapters ago, I told you about the origins of econometrics and the input-output model of the economy. Now I want you to think a bit about a ripple model.

The ripple model of economics and business is based on the idea that the best investment ideas don't necessarily come from the direct connections you can make, but rather, from indirect connections. For example, when you are looking at the sales of personal computers, you are also looking at the sales of the components inside those computers: the monitors, the hard drives, the integrated circuits. And when you are looking at those, you are also looking at the machinery that made the components—the wafer cutting and etching machines, the glass casting machinery that makes picture tubes, the makers of wire and capacitors—as well as the raw materials that went into the computers. So when you see the sales of personal computers rise or fall, you are not just looking at the results as they impact half a dozen personal-computer manufacturers, but rather, how those sales ripple outward all the way to a distant factor: the price of gold.

What does the price of gold have to do with the sale of personal computers? Inside your PC, there are dozens of memory chips and specialized integrated circuits, as well as a microprocessor. All of these have pin connectors so that the chips can receive the electricity that powers the computer, to start the flow of electrons along their circuit pathways. Those connectors are gold plated. The more computers that are sold, the more chips; the more chips, the more connectors; and the more connectors, the more gold that is used. Much of that gold is recovered from older computers and electronic components that have been scrapped; but generally, if demand is rising, then the supply has to rise as well, or the price goes up. So when you are checking out the personal-computer market, look at South African gold shares, because there might be a connection. The relative market shares among computer makers might not change at all, and their stock prices might remain flat; but if you can find the ripple effect between those computers and something else that *does* change, you have found a potentially relevant investment story.

You have to look for ripples. If you go outside and look at your backyard, all you are going to see is grass and trees and some flowers. But there is also a huge ecology of soil and insects and birds and small animals in your backyard, and if you fail to see that as well, then you've missed out on the ability to see something larger than what is just in front of you. Often, it is in seeing what others missed that the greatest ideas come along. I've always loved the story about a world-famous biologist who was asked by a colleague what he had done during his just-completed monthlong vacation. "Went exploring." When asked, "How far did you get?" he replied, "Halfway across the backyard."

I'm not suggesting that you are going to become any wiser by learning to stretch your mind by looking for the ripple effects, but I will bet that your conversations will become a lot more interesting. And every now and then, you will come up with a real investment winner.

Let's go back to personal computers for a moment. A couple of years ago, Intel, which makes microprocessors, figured out that a computer—from its perspective—was just a microprocessor with a bunch of other parts to help the processor work. So it persuaded computer makers to put "Intel Inside" labels on their computers. It was a brilliant strategy because it made everyone suddenly aware that a part of the computer could be as important as the whole—or even more important. As a result, Intel's stock zoomed upward, while the stocks of the computer makers languished. What Intel had done was to steal the brand value away from the computer makers and transfer that value to itself. By doing so, Intel made itself more valuable to investors.

Usually, this trick can be done only once, successfully, before the victim catches on. A couple of years after Intel launched its campaign, Seagate Technology, which manufactures disk drives, attempted a branding campaign of its own, and launched a series of television ads aimed at getting consumers to demand Seagate disk drives in their personal computers. But the manufacturers balked at putting yet another label on their boxes, and Seagate was forced to back down. On the other hand, another company, Iomega, repackaged its disk drives in jazzy cases, sold them as external drives, and saw its stock price go through the roof for a while.

We can learn some valuable lessons from these two examples. First, learn to look at simple items as components of more complex systems. When you purchase a can of peas, they are the end product of a huge agribusiness complex, and you should learn to look at what rising or falling sales mean to the components of that set of businesses. For example, are sales of pesticides rising or falling? Where are sales of farm equipment heading? What about hybrid and genetically modified seeds? (We noticed this effect in April 1999, and warned our readers about growing European resistance to Monsanto's genetically modified seeds. That resistance soon translated into an order ban by Archer-Daniels-Midland to its suppliers to segregate buying any corn grown from the seeds, and later on food-company bans on processing foods made from the crops grown with the seeds. You can see how the ripple effect works.) If you see your can of peas as the end product of a rippling chain, you will see all sorts of opportunities emerge.

Learning to look at the world as a series of chains or ripples is useful because you will find that the chains are not straight, but rather, kinked. During the Great Depression, when massive government intervention was needed to rescue the economy, all sorts of rules and practices were embedded into the supply and production chain, many of which continue to exist today. It is only in the last ten to fifteen years that many of these rules have been stripped away, and business is still adjusting to the changes. Many of the business deals you read about, from mergers and acquisitions to Internet start-ups and business-to-business Internet exchanges, have come into being as a result of attempts to rearrange value within the supply and production chain. Many companies would not exist if these chains did not need to be straightened out. For example, companies like SAP and Oracle would be relatively minor software vendors instead of giants if there were not a huge demand for straightening out and managing the supply chain better. Both companies make what are called "information backbones," complex programs that manage other programs and databases, and allow a company to integrate the software that controls inventory with the software that does the company's accounting or ordering. The need for these backbones is so great that SAP stock rose more than 200 percent between March 1999 and March 2000 as companies scrambled to straighten out their supply chains. Conversely, as those problems are ironed out of systems, companies will have to find new markets to add value to the companies they serve, or they will be replaced by other firms that can increase productivity in a different way.

Second, learn to look along value chains for areas of opportunity. You can assume that when an item is sold, its price reflects all of the markups that each component of the supply chain added to it. For example, a dress shirt might have about $1 worth of cotton in it, and a couple of pennies' worth of dye, for the raw materials. The fabric manufacturer who bought the raw cotton from a farmer or a farm commodities dealer will take the cotton and turn it into manufactured cloth, and mark it up, selling it for perhaps $2 a yard wholesale. The shirtmaker might take that fabric and turn it into a shirt and mark it up again, selling the shirt for

$8 to a wholesaler who, in turn, will sell it to a retailer for $16, who will sell it to the consumer for $32. You, as a marketplace checker, come along and look at the sale of men's shirts, and you see that there are lots of sales of premium shirts going on, and that the average selling price of shirts has risen to $40.

Who is earning that extra $8? Is it all going to Ralph Lauren and Calvin Klein and other upmarket brands, or is some of it finding its way down to the fabric manufacturer or the shirt factories in Malaysia and Sri Lanka, or to the farmer who is growing a better grade of cotton? If you can find out the answers, you will know who is experiencing the best margin expansion. That is where the investment opportunities are, if at least some of the companies are publicly traded.

2. Do other people know what you know? You may decide that *Titanic* is going to be really hot, the most profitable picture in history. It's meaningless if the rest of the world thinks the same thing. If you've read something in any general-interest publication—a newspaper, *Time, Newsweek, Forbes, Business Week,* for example—then it's already too well known for you to use. On the other hand, you might be reading *Linn's Stamp News* and see an article about a new kind of lamp that reduces eyestrain. If so, you may be seeing something that is early on the trend curve. This is especially true if the lamp can be used for other purposes. If it's good just for helping philatelists look at stamps, the upside will be limited. But if the lamps have applications to reduce eyestrain at the workplace, the sky's the limit.

If you read only the national newspapers and news-magazines, you probably didn't notice that there was a protest by Wisconsin dairy farmers in the spring of 2000 to protest low milk prices. If you had, as an investor with marketplace savvy, you would have translated that fact into cheap butterfat prices. Companies like Dean Foods (and ice-cream makers like Kraft, which

owns Breyers and Sealtest, and Unilever, which owns Ben &
Jerry's) benefit directly from low butterfat prices.

We talked about this earlier, when I was telling you about information sources, but it is worth amplifying here. You use marketplace checks to find information that other people don't
have—or, at least, that a sufficiently small number of people
have—so that it may not have already been factored into the decisions of most investment professionals. As you dig deeper and
deeper, you are going to move farther and farther away from the
sources you are familiar with, and toward sources that are private or exclusive. You are not going to become a spy and receive
secret information in dead drops, but you are going to work very
hard to cultivate the people who actually control the buying and
selling processes of this country, or the experts who observe and
analyze that process. *In order to do that, you have to learn to look
away from conventional sources, because conventional sources
contain conventional, received wisdom.*

What is your starting point for finding information that is
likely to be unknown? First ask, "Unknown by whom?" If it is the
Wall Street analyst community, you're going to have to dig pretty
deep, indeed, because Wall Street's analysts are paid handsomely
to remain on top of their chosen fields. The fact that they spend
most of their time doing financial modeling does not mean that
they are ignorant of what is going on in their fields. Rather, it
tends to mean that they discount most information as marginal,
until it becomes important.

Here's what I mean: Let's say that you are a restaurant analyst. While the total amount spent on eating out in the United
States is over $500 billion, that amount is divided among more
than one million restaurants. A large restaurant like Ivar's in
Seattle or Zehnders of Frankenmuth, in rural Michigan, might
do $20 million or more in annual revenues, but neither are
public companies; so no matter how well or how poorly they do,
the results are not going to move the needle for an analyst.

Instead, the analyst will look at sales of the half dozen or so large restaurant companies—McDonald's, Wendy's, Triarc (which owns Taco Bell, Pizza Hut, and KFC), and a handful of others. They might also include Diageo plc, which owns Burger King, because Burger King is such a large revenue contributor. Among that handful of companies, there are about $100 billion of sales, or 20 percent of all dining-out revenues, and perhaps 100,000 restaurants. So 10 percent of the restaurants account for 20 percent of the sales, which means that the remaining 90 percent account for only 80 percent of sales. Every dollar of revenues at one of the big, publicly traded companies is worth about $1.30 of a competitor's revenues.

Does this mean that you should simply ignore other restaurant chains? The answer is a resounding no. While McDonald's, Burger King, and Wendy's dominate overall, there are many local market disparities. In California, companies like In and Out Burger (still privately held but cutting edge as far a innovations and service) do a very nice job of keeping the fast-food Big Three at bay. Out on the road, chains like Cracker Barrel Old Country Stores, which are big at truck stops, exist in a world all their own, without much competition from the Big Three.

So it pays to disaggregate. When you look at the restaurant market as a whole, you are looking at an aggregated market, but if you break the market down into segments, the same way that the analysts break it down, you are disaggregating the market so that you can make more meaningful comparisons. You want to be able to compare like to like, so if you are looking at Cracker Barrel Old Country Stores (CBRL Group), you also want to be looking at Bob Evans Farms and Applebee's, two other publicly traded companies in the same space, in order to make comparisons that are meaningful.

This process of disaggregation has two advantages: First, by examining a smaller segment, you can look at it in greater detail. News means more in a smaller segment, so that if a new entrant into a segment appears, you can begin to examine exactly what that might mean, instead of looking at it as nothing more than a speck on the entire restaurant segment.

Second, examining a smaller slice of the market means that you are more likely to find a piece of information that Wall Street doesn't know. Most of the analysts will be covering the Big Three or, at most, five or six companies, and will look upon other segments as not meaningful. But if you follow a segment carefully, you can find those little ripples I mentioned earlier. If you are reading the restaurant trade publications, you will begin to have a pretty good idea of what is hot in the segment you are following; and then, if you can make friends with one of the editors, you may begin to get some bits of information sent your way.

Moreover, if you see a new restaurant in your area that fits into your category, you can begin to ask some questions: "Is it part of a national chain, or is it local?" "Is it having an impact on the segment that I am following in my geographic area?" "Is it likely to have an impact on revenues in other areas?"

Also, when you follow companies in a more detailed way, you are sometimes witnessing the birth of new stars. For example, Cracker Barrel was once just a local store in the rural South, and then it became a regional chain, and then it went superregional, went public, and expanded nationally. If you had been following it when it was not yet a public company, and had gotten to know the management, you would have known that the stock was a good buy at the time the company's IPO came out. Even if you had waited as long as 1990, when the company's sales were still a paltry $225 million, you would have made more money than you would have if you had simply bought the stock on a broker's recommendation.

Before the stock finally leveled off in 1998, it had risen more than 200 percent because it offered a lot of features that fast-food restaurants didn't: full, varied menus, lots of items besides food (like handcrafts and take-along food such as cheeses and candy) that you could also purchase, and presence along the interstates, so that if you were traveling a long distance, you could stop and rest for a while. (Every Cracker Barrel had a row of rocking chairs on its front porch.) Many people feel California's In and Out Burger falls into this category of future star.

Since we just mentioned IPOs, let's talk a little bit about technology stocks. Over the past two or three years, some huge fortunes have been made in the stock market in the run-up of shares following the initial public offerings of high-technology companies, especially Internet and wireless telecommunication stocks. In 1999, Qualcomm, a wireless company and Broadvision, an Internet software company, were the two hottest companies in the stock market, both posting gains well in excess of 500 percent. If you had been prescient, you would have bought both stocks on their opening trade, made a large fortune, and retired. But you probably didn't, and you probably missed most of the technology rise, as most people did. You missed it because you couldn't separate the winners from the losers. This is of particular importance for people who invested in the first half of 2000. Much of the sector was battered. If you had marketplace insights, you had the opportunities to pick up some of the long-term winners, and avoid the permanent losers.

Wall Street's analysts can't choose the winners very well, either. What institutional money managers do is take the recommendations of sector analysts and then buy the entire sector. If wireless stocks are suddenly hot, they buy every single wireless stock, and begin to sell them off only when the sector begins to cool down. After a relatively short time—anywhere from a couple of months to about a year—the winners begin to separate themselves from the losers, the companies that have good strategies from the underachievers. At that point, institutional investors begin to ruthlessly dump the companies they perceive as weak.

187

That's a tough strategy for you to follow. You are not in Silicon Valley, having breakfast with venture capitalists at Buck's restaurant in Woodside, or listening to investment bankers making deals over lunch and lattes at Il Fornaio in Palo Alto. You have no access to the buzz about what is hot, and even if you are reading the latest issue of *The Industry Standard,* the magazine that is most widely read among the Silicon Valley community, you are still going to be weeks behind.

So read the *Standard,* but then go out and do your research and look for the best companies based on everything you've learned so far. Buy a couple of companies in the same sector, such as wireless, and concentrate on those. It will force you to become knowledgeable. By concentrating on a few companies, you will be more expert about them, more likely to find the next winner before Wall Street does.

3. Will it happen reasonably quickly? This is the counterargument of the one above. For the most part, you will be digging for information that nobody else has. Then what? If that information never comes to light, it will never have an impact on stock prices. In the long run, almost every investment theory is right in some way. But, how long can you afford to wait? If you are going to outsmart Wall Street, you have to have a pretty good idea that what you have learned is going to become known to others relatively soon, usually before the next quarter's earnings reports. So if you find a bit of information that helps you buy early or sell early, you have to be prepared to act on it. If that new lamp you saw in the stamp magazine is going to be in development for another three years, pass it by. The same is true for miracle cures from drug companies, and many new technologies. All of them float along on a wave of buzz and hype; your job as a marketplace checker is to separate fact from fancy, and to find the facts that are going to have impact soon.

Finally, remember to put what you have learned into context. Marketplace research is important, but it is only a piece of the puzzle. You need to know what the other pieces of the puzzle look like. What is the general consensus on Wall Street about your company? Why do they think differently from you? You may discover that the main product of a company is losing market share; yet, when you track the stock, you see that the share price is rising every week.

For a while in August 2000, that's exactly what was happening to Novell, a maker of computer-networking software. There were persistent rumors that the company was going to be taken over by IBM, and it pushed the depressed shares up 33 percent in about two weeks. It wasn't until the end of August, when the company announced layoffs, that the shares began to back down to their prerumor level.

If the stock is gaining because the analysts are buying the company's claims that the product is selling well, then you have something to grab hold of and make money from. On the other hand, the company might be the subject of a takeover rumor, and the stock price is reacting to that. Then it really doesn't matter whether you are right or wrong. The price of the stock is being dictated by rumor, not by the forces of the marketplace. This happens, and while I believe that in the long run marketplace results are reflected in stock prices, it doesn't help you if you lose your money before your marketplace-check strategy takes hold. So I'll show you some checks that will keep you from making bad decisions based on good information.

These are really pretty simple. There is already a lot of information on the Internet, at sites such as TheStreet.com, and CBS.MarketWatch.com, that can tell you about insider buying and selling. Insiders are not supposed to trade on material information before that information is released to the general public, but there is a large gray area of what constitutes insider trading.

If I work at a company, but I have not seen any documents indicating that a takeover is in the works, but my own knowledge of the company tells me that the company is ripe to be taken over, my buying or selling of my company's stock is not insider trading.

On the other hand, if I am an officer of the company, and I have been part of the discussions, or I have signed off on any of the documents, I am not supposed to trade on my knowledge. Because there is so much gray space in who knows what and who is allowed to act on it, several services constantly track and watch to see if company insiders are buying or selling their own company's stock. If they are buying, that is generally a statement of belief that the company is on the verge of doing better. If they are selling, it is generally an indication that the company is on the verge of doing worse. Of course, if a founder has 95 percent of his net worth tied up in company stock, it is prudent financial planning to diversify his portfolio no matter how good the prospects for his company.

12

THE TEN IMMUTABLE LAWS OF MARKETPLACE CHECKING

Now that you know the how and the why of marketplace checks, it will be easier for you to understand what we call the immutable laws of the system. These are the ten rules that we live by at Off the Record Research. They are the tests we give to every piece of information that comes to us. These are simple, commonsense tests. None of them require any kind of statistical knowledge or advanced academic training. They will help you search out better-quality information on companies you might invest in, to help you achieve better returns.

Law #1: Where You Are on the Bell Curve Matters

There is a life cycle to events, products, and even companies. Where you are in the life cycle will often determine your investment decision. For example, pain relief has been an industry since aspirin was first commercialized in the 1880s. For nearly a century, aspirin was the sole nonnarcotic analgesic. Then came acetaminophen, the active ingredient in Tylenol. It eliminated many of the side effects that aspirin sometimes caused, like upset stomach and intestinal bleeding in patients with ulcers, or Reye's syndrome in children. Tylenol, in turn, has been crowded in the marketplace by ibuprofen, which is the ingredient found in Motrin, Advil, Ibren, Ifen, and Profen. In turn, ibuprofen has been squeezed by the naproxens, such as Aleve.

Now come Cox-2 inhibitors, a new class of drugs, which are extremely effective in relieving severe pain, like the pain that accompanies rheumatoid arthritis and osteoarthritis. Monsanto's Celebrex and Merck's Vioxx are rapidly becoming the new standard for treating severe arthritis pain, and it seems to be only a matter of time before the Cox-2 drugs are used for other forms of pain relief.

So if you look at all of those drugs and plotted where they were on a curve whose start and end points were zero—in other words, an ordinary bell curve—you'd see that aspirin was very far over to the right in terms of its life cycle, and the Cox-2 inhibitors were very far over to the left, right at the beginning of their life cycle.

Where you are on the curve often translates into how you invest. Tylenol is Johnson & Johnson's biggest single product in terms of sales, and one of their most profitable. As each additional pain medication squeezes Tylenol's market share, J&J is forced to find other products to make up for the shrinking revenues and profits that are coming from Tylenol. One of these is J&J's own Cox-2 drug, Remicade, but there are currently concerns about its cost, and the fact that it has to be administered intravenously by a doctor. Newer products generally translate into more significant sales gains, and older products, even if they are quite profitable, require ever-increasing amounts of advertising to hold their market share. That reduces their profitability and makes them—and the companies that produce them—less attractive over time.

Do old products get new lives? Aspirin had 100 percent of the pain market to itself for nearly a century. Now it has barely 10 percent. But that percentage has lately been growing again, with the evidence that an aspirin taken at the beginning of chest pains may be instrumental in halting an oncoming heart attack. Given that aspirin is cheap and that heart attacks are a leading cause of death, keeping a couple of bottles of aspirin around—in your glove compartment, on your boat, in your office and your home—is inexpensive insurance against the possibility of a sudden heart attack.

Often, you aren't looking at a product when you are looking at a trend, but an entire industry, or a phenomenon. The current suburban-housing boom began right after World War II, with the construction of the first Levittown, on Long Island. That was followed by decades of suburban sprawl, and the construction of literally tens of millions of housing units. For much of the past fifty years, the needs of homeowners were supplied adequately by house-and-garden shops, nurseries, hardware stores, and lumberyards.

But beginning in the late 1970s, two events changed the way people bought things for their homes. First, inflation forced the price of nearly everything through the roof. Second, as the oldest homes began to age, they needed more than just an occasional repair. People in the 1970s who were buying homes built in the 1940s and 1950s discovered, to their chagrin, that the walls on their homes were often brittle, and when they wanted to hammer in a nail or picture hook, they were left with a large hole. They could plaster the hole over, or they could re-Sheetrock the entire house. Likewise, when they pulled down the old Sheetrock, they discovered that the old wiring was fraying or, worse, made of aluminum, and needed to be replaced.

With home-repair needs growing and costs rising, it was natural that somebody would come up with a home-repair superstore that bought in sufficient volume to be able to offer deep discounts to strapped homeowners, who, because of high costs, were increasingly forced to do projects like rewiring and deck building by themselves. The do-it-yourself movement took off in the 1970s, and has shown absolutely no sign of letting up anytime soon. If anything, as people gain some experience with doing major home projects, gain the tools they need to be able to tackle such projects, and lose their fears, they take on larger and larger projects, such as laying floors and building entire additions. So stores like Home Depot and Lowe's are enjoying some of their best years ever, even though they are relatively far along in their life cycle. And, because new homes are not being built at the rates that they were in the period between 1945 and 1970, it is likely that home remodeling and repair will be an industry that continues to grow for years to come.

One more example will serve to underscore how important it is to pay attention to the life cycles of products, companies, and markets. Until 2000, sales of products at Staples and Office Depot were humming along, but there are now some trouble signs on the horizon. Many people we spoke with told us that both companies were getting an increasing share of their revenues from the sale of personal computers. If that is so, then any downturn in PC sales will have a significant impact on the companies. In fact, during late September and early October, 1999, PC inventories were low, and that indeed hampered sales.

But that is only a blip. What might be far more important is the fact that despite all the hype about dot-com start-ups, the rate of new business start-ups is slowing for the first time since the late 1970s. We are in the midst of a full-employment boom, so there just aren't very many people around to form new businesses. Moreover, if you had to choose between starting your own small business and joining one which was a well-financed venture start-up, which would you choose? Most people are lured by the prospect of a big stock-market reward, and choose the well-financed venture start-up. With small-business start-ups lagging, that means that the market for office-supply stores might be moving towards saturation and it is altogether possible that the industry could consolidate.

So it is important to pay attention to the curve. Generally, the farther along a company or a product is in its life cycle, the harder it is to get the kind of double-digit growth you need for a great investment. How does this all boil down? Generally, drug companies are good investments when they are pushing new products into the pipeline. The large home-remodeling stores are good investments when interest rates don't choke off sales, and office superstores are good as long as new-business formation continues to rise. When any of those trends change, the investment possibilities of those categories begin to decline.

Law #2: The Information Must Be Material to Your Investment Decision

What is materiality? Here is an example: You go into your local Kmart and notice that 3M's new tape, which is in a roll that fits your hand, so you can wrap presents and pull off precut strips of adhesive, is selling like gangbusters. You do some quick calculations and figure that every household will surely buy two or three rolls of this tape, at 79 cents per roll. At 100 million households, that could mean as much as $240 million in sales for 3M. It sounds good—but what are the facts, really?

First, not every household will buy one roll, let alone three. New-product adoption rates are slow, so it might be just *half* the households, and they might buy only one roll. That brings the potential sales down to $40 million.

But that's at retail. Assuming that 3M sells its products to Kmart and Wal-Mart and other stores at the usual 40 percent wholesale cost, the company brings in only $16 million in revenues. In 2000 3M reported sales of over $16.5 billion. The new tape's contribution: about 0.1 percent. Such a small increase in sales is not material to 3M's top line, let alone its bottom line. Now, 3M is an innovative company with a reputation for bringing out lots of new products all the time. Therefore, for you to look seriously at 3M, you have to look around to find if there are lots of new products coming out. If there are, you have a probable winner.

For a product to be material, its sales or profits have to have a dramatic and deep impact on a company's bottom line. Campbell sells several hundred different kinds of soup, so no one soup product matters much in the mix. But if soup consumption overall drops because of an unusually warm winter or a shift in dietary habits, that is a material drop. Many companies attempt to broaden and diversify their product lines in an attempt to defeat materiality. No CEO wants his livelihood to depend upon only a single product, but product proliferation creates other problems. The more products you have (SKUs or store-keeping units, in the language of retailers), the greater the likelihood that you won't get all of them onto every retailer's shelves, and the greater the possibility that you will have to manage inventory as well as you manage production.

Introducing new products is expensive. In addition to the marketing expense, there are expenses that come from additional levels of complexity—your computer inventory system has to handle more entries, your warehouse has to pick and pack more different varieties, you have to maintain more varied production lines, or have multiple outsourcing contracts—and all of these translate to increased operating costs.

You may find that the growth or death of any given product is not material to a company's overall health, but materiality can be like the old torture of a thousand cuts: a poorly performing product here, one there, and pretty soon it adds up to real money. The converse is also true: Like 3M's tape, it doesn't amount to much, but if the company also adds a lot of other products, and each of them posts a small but solid profit, then the company's prospects improve.

There used to be something called the Cockroach Theory of Investing. If you see one cockroach on your floor, you know that there are thousands more in the walls. The same is true with materiality. You might see one badly behaving product, but can it give you clues that there are others? Well, you should certainly start looking at more products made by the company, and looking back to the balance sheet. Look at the lines labeled "cost of goods sold" and "selling, general and administrative expenses." If either or both of those are rising faster than sales, then you know there is a problem.

Conversely, a nonmaterial product may be the start of a trend. Let's go back to 3M. When the company introduced Post-it notes in the 1980s, nobody could have foreseen that those sticky little pieces of yellow paper would become a major product for 3M. Yet they now come in 29 colors, 56 shapes, 27 sizes and account for hundreds of millions of dollars in annual sales. Twenty years ago, Post-its weren't material. Today they are, and 3M works very hard to find new uses for Post-its to keep sales growing.

Where should you look for materiality? Electronics hardware and computers are two industries where new-product introductions can have a material effect on sales. When Intel introduces a new chip that ships in quantity, it can change the dynamics of the computer marketplace as everyone rushes to be the first to incorporate the chip into their new computers. Similarly, Apple Computer is a company whose market share lives and dies by its ability to introduce new products.

Another industry where materiality counts is entertainment. Huge entertainment conglomerates like Disney and AOL Time Warner have many different products, so it's a question of which products are material. The best-selling book will make only a negligible impact on the sales of either company; the *same is true* for a hit television show like *Monday Night Football* for Disney or *The Sopranos* for Time Warner. But a blockbuster movie like *Titanic,* which grossed more than $1 billion worldwide, or *Star Wars,* which will do about the same, can be highly material to an entertainment conglomerate's fortunes. Of course, you have to know how the money is going to be divided up, but generally, the bigger the box-office gross, the more money that lands on the doorstep of the company that distributes it and the studio that produces it.

Law #3: Don't Get Fooled by the Village Venus

In medieval times, when travel was uncommon, every village had at least one girl whom everyone believed was a ravishing beauty. She could have been ugly; but in the absence of any means of comparison, she was the Village Venus, and she held her title until the first country fair, at which point she might have triumphed as the fairest of the fair, or gone home as just another pockmarked face. As more people traveled farther, and as photography and then movies and television reached into every village and home, the level of the standard of beauty continued to rise, to an international standard.

The same is true of trends, products, and companies. You might be living in farm country in Iowa. You notice that everyone is wearing overalls, so you might be fooled into thinking that everyone everywhere wears overalls. They don't. A quick trip into a nearby town that's at least twice the size of your own community will suddenly confirm that a good number of people never wear overalls, so the "trend" that you think you've spotted goes right out the window.

The Village Venus is a trap that anyone can fall into. You get enamored of an idea or a concept because it is novel to you, and you forget to check whether it is novel to anyone else. One of the great advantages of developing an extended group—one made up of people outside your own local area—is that you can quickly check your own perceptions against the perceptions of people in other parts of the country. So, if you go on-line with your group, and you find that teenage girls in Los Angeles and New York are all wearing overalls, along with the farmers of Iowa, you might have spotted a trend.

It also matters who is doing the wearing. For years, the bicycle messengers of midtown Manhattan wore short, tight-fitting Lycra shorts. No one took notice until fashion models in the garment center began to copy the look. Suddenly it became a worldwide fashion trend. At that point, you need to get some better confirmation, in the form of finding some retail buyers to add to your panel. Start asking people in your group if they know retail buyers around the country, either through friends or relatives, and then set up a serious research panel to check out your finding. If you do that, you'll rarely be blinded by the beauty of the idea in front of you.

Law #4: Facts Have to Have Staying Power

One of the questions we're always asking at Off the Record Research is, "Does what we know have staying power? Is it a trend or a fad?" For example, when we find out that doctors are prescribing more Lipitor, an anticholesterol medicine, instead of Zocor, that would tend to shift the balance from Merck, which makes Zocor, to Pfizer, which makes Lipitor. But we have to know whether the shift is the result of heavy advertising and marketing expenditures—drug companies spend billions of dollars not only in advertising, but in wining and dining doctors and taking them to exotic locations for conferences, in hopes of persuading them to change the drugs they prescribe—or whether there is real clinical evidence that one drug is better than another.

Even then, there can be extraneous factors. For example, many emergency-room physicians and cardiologists who began practice a decade ago marveled at the ability of Genentech's +PA to stop a heart attack in mid-course. As a result, though there are newer, more effective drugs available, they stick with +PA over other therapies, making it difficult for newer drugs to make inroads.

That is what we mean by staying power. Often, being the first into the market with a very good product can gain you an unassailable No. 1 position. In a 1994 study by London-based Interbrand Corp., the strongest brands in England in 1933 were still the market leaders in 1994, more than sixty years later. Hoover was still No. 1 in vacuum cleaners. (In fact, Britons don't vacuum their carpets and floors, they "Hoover" them.) Colgate was still No. 1 in toothpaste, Gillette was still No. 1 in razors, Cadbury was still No. 1 in chocolates.

The U.S. market is much the same.

Despite huge changes in distribution, despite huge changes in consumption patterns brought about by demographic and geographic shifts, most dominant brands in the United States have been No. 1 for many years. Kodak is still the best-selling film. Gillette is still No. 1 in razor blades. Kellogg's is still the No. 1 cereal maker.

Few competitors have ever been able to destroy a strong brand. Generally, it takes a catastrophe to kill off a brand. Even then, as with the Tylenol poisoning scare of nearly three decades ago—a person, to this day unknown, replaced Tylenol capsules with capsules laced with cyanide, killing several people—a company can rescue a brand with the proper action. J&J recalled all the Tylenol it had sold, replaced it with new Tylenol which was produced with a sealed packaging system, and made its products increasingly tamperproof.

When you observe the sales of a product rising and falling, you have to get more facts. If it is a consumer product, ask your panel members if there has been heavy couponing for the product in their area. If the answer is no, ask if there have been lots of store promotions. Often, manufacturers work out deals with supermarkets and discount stores wherein they will deliver a much larger volume of goods at a steep discount in return for a heavy store promotion of those goods. That is what is known as "push" marketing, because the goods are literally pushed through the distribution system to the consumer.

If sales have been rising but there does not seem to be any apparent promotion, start asking other questions. Has a given product added new options? For example, if Campbell comes up with a whole new range of soups that contain roasted garlic, and that's a taste that everyone likes, then sales will take off among those new soups, with or without promotion. Since companies depend to a certain extent on word of mouth to spread good news about their products—one satisfied customer will tell ten friends, of whom five will try the product, and so on—then you should depend upon word of mouth as well. Find out if there is any "buzz" about what appears to be a hot-selling product. Ask the members of your group if they have heard anything out of the ordinary, and keep asking until you find a reason. If there is no reason, you generally don't have a basis for decision.

Law #5: Facts Without a Hypothesis Are Useless

That brings us to our next important rule. Nothing happens in a vacuum, so if you can't find the reason that something is happening, the fact that it is happening is useless to you in making an investment decision. Anytime our reporters come to us with an observation, we ask them to come up with a workable hypothesis which might account for the facts. Then we go out and test the hypothesis.

For example, around the beginning of August 1999, after noticing a lack of candy at my local Walgreen's, we began hearing rumors that there was a chocolate shortage, and that the candy companies were going to have trouble shipping candy for Halloween. Sure enough, when we began checking up, we found that overall, shipments at all of the companies were down, but retailers kept telling us that they were down more for Hershey Foods than for other manufacturers, such as Mars, Inc.

Since Hershey is one of the world's largest buyers of chocolate, we began to suspect that something else was amiss, so we told our reporter to begin making some calls to candy buyers and to test the chocolate-shortage hypothesis. In talking to four different buyers who bought for more than 7,000 stores we found out that Hershey Foods had internal problems which made it more difficult for it to ship goods. The company had made a significant investment in new SAP inventory management and billing software, and that software was plagued with problems. As a result, the company literally couldn't get orders out the door, leading to a year-to-year decrease in sales during September 1999. Buyers said that the problems were ongoing and, as a result, sales by competitors Nestlé S.A., Mars, Inc., and Russell Stover were on the rise.

As a nonprofessional, you might think that such information is hidden from you, but it isn't. Remember the film, *Six Degrees of Separation?* The theory that we all exist within six degrees of separation of each other has been proved mathematically, and it is a powerful bit of information for you to remember when you are attempting to secure information. When you are trying to confirm a hypothesis, talk to your panel and ask them to ask every friend or relative who might have an insight. If the answer comes back that they know no one, ask them to ask those friends and relatives to ask all of their friends and relatives. Usually, within one or two tries, you will come up with the right person.

Use your imagination to confirm a hypothesis. In the Hershey's case, you had your choice of someone in the company, candy buyers, or even, if you had discovered that Hershey Foods was having trouble with SAP software, finding someone in SAP who might be able to give you some hints. There are also always rumors floating around in trade publications, so make it your business to find the editors of the publications which cover the industries you are following, and then don't be shy about calling them up and sharing information. If you tell them that you have heard and confirmed some rumors about Hershey's shipping problems, they will make some phone calls, assign a reporter, and call you back with the information that there is indeed an inventory-management software problem.

Of course, in order to confirm a hypothesis, you have to be willing to expose your theory to the harsh light of reality. You have to share it with someone, who will either amplify it or shoot it down. In a very important way, it does not matter if your hypothesis is right or wrong. If it is correct, your contact will tell you so and amplify it, providing the additional information that helps you quickly determine if what you are observing represents a trend or a fad. If the expert to whom you explain your hypothesis shoots down your theory, chances are that he or she will provide a better explanation which accounts for the facts, and give you a much firmer foundation upon which to make decisions.

Law #6: Profit from the Law of Unintended Consequences

Almost every event has a ripple effect on the economy and on your investment decisions, much the way a stone thrown into a pond causes concentric circles of ripples on the pond's surface. In investing, the ripples are sometimes expected; but often, things happen that we don't quite understand until afterward. If you can learn to remember that *unexpected* events are the norm, and learn to be on the lookout for them, you can actually make a lot of money when you invest.

One way to think about secondary effects is to look at such things as the outcome of the Law of Unintended Consequences, which says that nobody is smart enough to really think through the implications of the decisions they make. An easy way to understand the Law of Unintended Consequences is to look at a chessboard. The average player can "look ahead" about three moves. If you move your queen, you can envision what your opponent's next most logical response will be, figure out your next move and your opponent's logical response, and the move after that.

And that's it. Since the average game lasts thirty to forty moves, you are almost always in the dark about the next set of outcomes, and have to be extremely cautious from about the fourth move onward.

Here's an example of an unintended secondary effect: Remember our example of Home Depot in Law #1? As the size, scale, and scope of home-remodeling and repair projects has continued to grow, they have unexpectedly changed the nature of finance in the United States. Only a decade ago, you might go into your local bank and ask for a home-improvement loan, and your bank might lend you up to $10,000 to renovate your kitchen.

But new kitchens can cost up to $100,000, today, so what do you do? You get a home-equity loan. You borrow back the money you've already used to pay down your mortgage, and you add to the value of your home, in the hope that you'll get the money back when you sell. The home-equity loan industry didn't even exist in the early 1970s, and now it is a multibillion-dollar giant, and is growing larger every day. But it would not exist if there had not been a rise in the market for home improvements, and the rise of retailers like Home Depot.

Do you see? A growth in one industry can cause a growth in another. Often, a small change in one industry can cause a much larger change in a secondary market. Computers were supposed to usher in the paperless office. Instead, once the price of computer-driven printers came down, there was an explosion in the demand for paper. As a consequence, paper prices have been rising steadily for over a decade, even as new capacity has been added. Moreover, paper has ceased being a commodity product. The new laser printers demand higher-performance papers, which are more expensive, leading to rising profits for the papermakers.

Secondary effects are all around you. Let's stay in the computer area for a while longer. In 1987, there were about 30 million personal computers in the United States, and about another 15 million in the rest of the world. Almost all of them were in the office, and almost none of them were in the home. After the stock market crashed in 1987, large companies began to shed employees vigorously—it was called "downsizing."

Many of the people fired were extremely talented, and at the height of their careers. What did they do? They saw the falling prices of computers, printers, and other office equipment, and they went into business for themselves as a legion of consultants and advisors. Today the office is often in the home—according to *Home Office* magazine, there are more than 26 million home-based businesses—and there are more than 156 million computers in use in the United States, a seven-fold increase. The number continues to grow as people extend their enterprises into the 24 × 7 world of the Internet and need even more hardware and software.

Let's look at what might become another secondary effect. Sales of digital cameras have lately been increasing, as people get comfortable with downloading images onto their computers

205

and sending picture files of their children to their loved ones around the world. But what happens when you combine the increased use of digital cameras with the rising use of auction-based Web sites like eBay? If you want to sell merchandise, it helps to have a picture of it, and the easier it is to take a picture of the lamp you inherited from Aunt Agnes, the easier it is for you to sell. As soon as that idea catches on, the sale of digital cameras will explode.

Sometimes a secondary effect does not come from a shift in an industry, but a shift in demographic or social trends. For example, one of the largest single unintended consequences of the large number of women entering the labor market in the 1970s and 1980s was that it changed the character of the automobile market forever. Women didn't earn as much as men, so they needed smaller cars; and because they didn't know or want to know much about car repair, they demanded cars that were highly reliable. The Japanese stepped into the market to supply fleets of Toyotas and Nissans and Hondas, and the U.S. auto market changed. General Motors, which made big cars, saw its total market share erode from one-half to one-third of the market, because the company was slow to recognize women's need to be served.

Most businessmen think they can get a jump on unintended consequences. They like to envision scenarios—we do this, our competitors do that; we respond by doing such and such, and the market responds thusly—because it gives them comfort in doing their planning. For example, my marketing guru tells me that there is a product, let's say ice-cream bars, which accounts for about 10 percent of the ice-cream market, and there is only a single, undercapitalized company that makes all the ice-cream bars in the world. If I will listen to my marketing guru, I will get into the ice-cream-bar business and take a couple of share points away from my competitor. I research the market, find that the demand for ice-cream bars has been growing slowly each year, and

I don't see any evidence that another competitor has seen the same hole in the market that my marketing guru has found. So I go ahead and make the $30 million required investment in an ice-cream plant and get into the ice-cream-bar business. Soon I sell a pretty nice bar covered in thick, rich chocolate.

Two weeks later, right after my product hits the stores, the U.S. Surgeon General comes out with a report that says that chocolate causes cancer in laboratory mice. Suddenly, nobody wants to buy chocolate products anymore. My competitor, who also makes ice-cream sandwiches, can survive. Either I have to close my plant because I don't have the capacity to make ice-cream sandwiches, or I am forced to spend another $30 million to put in a baking line so I can make the sandwich components. If I still have a job, I'll probably shut the plant. Otherwise I'd have to charge about twice as much for my product as my competitor is charging, to amortize my additional costs. I did everything right, and I still lost, because of an unanticipated event that had a major consequence on the viability of my business.

That sort of thing happens all the time, and you have to learn to become aware of it, and how to take advantage of it when it happens. If you pick up a business magazine or *The Wall Street Journal,* and you read some business forecaster making a prediction about some aspect of business, you can assume that he or she is wrong at least 90 percent of the time. Almost all forecasts are straight-line projections, so if a business has been growing by 30 percent a year, the assumption is that it is going to keep growing at that rate until it absorbs all the capital in the world.

But anyone with a lick of common sense knows that if a business is growing at 30 percent annually, it is bound to attract new competitors the way a pot of honey attracts flies. That's where your opportunities arise. You can invest in the new competitors, with some assurance that at least one of them will prevail in the marketplace, or you can short the stock or buy put options of the market leader, on the assumption that the announcement of competition is going to have an adverse impact on the company's fortunes.

For example, in January 2000, there were no more than a handful of companies attempting to make and sell products that allowed cell phones to link to the Internet. By mid-2000, there were more than 200 such companies, all attempting to cash in on the idea that people might want to access the Internet through the tiny screens of their cell phones. According to *The Industry Standard,* one of the magazines that follows the new-technology economy, no more than a handful of companies will be likely winners out of the 200. Of these, only six—OmniSky, AvantGo, Phone.com, Aether Systems, InfoSpace, and Research in Motion—had sales under $100 million. All the rest were multibillion-dollar communications giants, like Lucent and Nortel Networks. The upside for the large companies might be good, but it is probably better for the small ones that already have some significant revenue and growth prospects.

Or, you can do things the OTR way and create a research panel that begins to keep track of the industry, so you can know with some certitude exactly who is going to come out on top.

Law #7: For Every Winner, There's a Loser

In many markets, demand is fairly constant, the market size is relatively fixed, and competitors are left to duke it out for share points. In this situation, my win is your loss, and vice versa. It's a zero-sum game.

Here are two examples from late October 1999. We reported that Republic Services Inc., a waste hauler, was picking up share at the expense of Waste Management Inc., by offering more personalized services and more competitive pricing. According to forty-nine buyers of services for large commercial and residential property-management companies we contacted, companies were turning to Republic Services because Waste Management was not willing to lower its prices, while Republic, which wanted to grow its business, was.

Second, we reported that two large railroads, CSX and Norfolk Southern, were losing market share to trucking companies. Large shippers reported experiencing traffic delays, freight losses, and freight-yard congestion because of Conrail's consolidation of the two lines' eastern rail networks, according to rail industry specialists we surveyed. According to our sources, the shippers were diverting between 3 percent and 7 percent of their shipments to trucking companies.

These two examples define the winner/loser paradigm perfectly. In garbage hauling, the market grows only as fast as the population grows, with slight additional growth coming from a better economy—people consume more and there is more new construction-site waste. It shrinks a bit when the economy tightens because people consume a little less. Because garbage collection is both capital intensive—each new garbage truck costs about $500,000—and labor intensive, companies grow only when there is the solid prospect of securing major additional business, like an entire municipality, or an office park. In addition, the business is constrained from growth by transportation costs—the garbage has to be taken somewhere for disposal—and tipping fees—you have to pay the dump owner money to take your garbage away—as well as increasingly strict environmental regulations.

All of these factors militate against large numbers of new competitors. In fact, if you were to look at the garbage industry, you would see that there has been a long, steady consolidation of local and regional companies into a few national enterprises. While there is still some share to be acquired by acquiring local or regional independents, most of the growth in the industry is gone.

Under those situations, you are looking at a pure winner/loser situation. If you develop an interest in these stocks, it is a simple enough job to monitor their growth. If you see that one of the companies has sales that are rising faster than the market as a whole, it is time to do a little research, with some foreknowledge of the outcome. If Republic is growing faster than the industry, then Allied Waste Industries or Waste Management is almost bound to be losing revenue or share. A couple of calls to property managers will help you confirm a winner/loser hypothesis, or tell you that Republic has just acquired a few additional local carters.

The same thing is true with the transport industry, except perhaps more so. The number of railroads has already consolidated from hundreds down to a handful, and the number of trucking companies has collapsed from thousands only twenty years ago to perhaps a couple of dozen very large players, with air freight and ocean shipping dominated by even fewer companies.

Package volume is entirely a function of the economic health of the nation. Each downturn causes vicious rate discounting among shipping companies, so that, at each upturn, there are yet fewer competitors. If you want to invest in trucking companies, you have to be prepared for the fact that each winner is going to make it that much harder on the remaining companies, and that there will be far more losers.

Another area where the winner/loser cycle is just emerging is electrical power generation. For more than a century, electrical power in the United States has been generated on a local or regional basis, with local companies granted monopolies by government bodies in return for fairly strict controls upon the pricing of power. But beginning in the late 1980s, power companies seeking a way out from under the crushing cost of pollution cleanup efforts began to ask regulators for permission to merge with competitors, both to produce entities which were, at least on paper, more environmentally friendly (e.g., a "clean" hydropower company might merge with a power company which produced most of its power from coal, and thereby beat the regulations) and use their larger combined rate base to gain cheaper borrowing rates for financing the cleanup.

As the power industry began to consolidate, regulators decided to deregulate, and to throw power consumption open to competition, which caused another round of consolidation. Within the space of a decade, almost half the local power companies in the United States have disappeared into mergers, and of those remaining at least half will disappear in another decade. As the winners gain more share, the losers will have little choice except to find a suitable merger partner, or find that they can no longer compete.

Law #8: Everything Is Relative

Here is a question for you: In 1997, Apple Computer was selling as low as $15 a share. In 1999, it was selling as high as $110 a share. That's a gain of more than 600 percent. When was the best time to get into Apple, and when was the best time to get out? Obviously, the best answer would have been to get in at the bottom and get out at the top. But without 20/20 hindsight, almost nobody knows what the real bottom is for a company with problems, or what the real top is for a company that is succeeding in the marketplace. Before World War I, if you had bought 1,000 shares of General Motors, you probably would have sold it during the depression of 1919–1921, which was called the Great Depression—until the depression of 1929–39 came along. On the other hand, if you'd held onto your General Motors through thick and thin, through stock splits and dividend increases, and reinvested all your dividends in more GM shares, you'd be a certified billionaire today.

The same thing is true if you had bought International Business Machines at about the same time, or Hewlett-Packard

211

or Microsoft when they first went public. Each company turned a modest investment into a handsome fortune for people who were willing to hold on for the long haul.

But that's not the way most investors behave. They grow impatient with their stocks if they don't see the kind of performance they expect, or if they hear a friend or neighbor bragging at the country club about some Internet stock that their broker or brother-in-law got them into. We're not advocating a buy-and-hold strategy here, we're merely pointing out that when you buy and when you sell has a lot to do with the performance of the stocks you own, and that it is very difficult, even for seasoned professional traders, to know exactly when to get in and when to get out.

This is where good research comes in. If you have developed your network adequately, you should have at least a one-quarter jump on the rest of the market in an upturn, and a less than one-quarter jump for a downturn.

Why? Market psychology. The market always believes that it is discounting all good news in advance, so it won't allow additional good news to move a stock until there are a couple of confirmatory pieces of information. In other words, if you are tracking the book-to-bill ratio of the semiconductor industry—how many new orders go on the books versus how many orders are filled—you might believe that one week's rise is good enough for you, and you might decide to jump into AMD or Intel right at that point.

But a seasoned trader will wait for a month or two to determine if that upward trend is consistent. If there is, the trader will talk to his company's semiconductor analyst, who might then issue a "buy" rating on the group, and cause a flood of institutional money to flow into those stocks and related issues. Institutions might miss the first five points of the rise, but they will grab almost all of the rest.

Conversely, when a market is beginning to flatten out, smart traders do not wait for a downturn to get out. They begin to look for "momentum." What is the slope of the curve? It might still be upward, but if each week brings a smaller gain than the one before, it won't be too long before a week comes along when sales are flat, or even down. Smart traders don't wait for the last rise of the curve. They are willing to leave a few dollars of stock price rise on the table for innocent individual investors, knowing full well that their controlled selling before the peak of the market will turn into share *dumping* as soon as everyone figures out that the market for semiconductors is going down and not up.

As a small investor with limited resources, you must determine where you are on the price curve for every stock you own. This is a critical lesson. Your resources are limited, so you want to have the best chance of capturing the *best* gain—not the *most* gain. Look for companies whose sales are just entering a rapid growth phase, and which are likely to continue growing for some time—at least, several quarters.

The expansion of sales, along with the expansion of earnings that usually accompanies such growth, provides Wall Street with the demand which drives an expansion of the price earnings multiple—how much Wall Street is willing to pay up for each incremental gain in earnings. The faster sales and earnings grow, the faster the multiple rises—a cycle that drives up stock prices. If you can find an entry point on the way up, and then use the methods you've learned in this book to monitor the companies in which you've invested, you'll be able to know when the momentum ride is over, and when Wall Street is about to bail out of your favorite stock.

Relativity is crucial in the research process itself. If you are following a company and its sales are up, does that make it a good investment? Maybe. But what if a competitor's sales are up more? So the question, "Compared to what?" must be asked. All companies sell their products against some sort of competition. Even if there is no direct competition, there is always indirect competition. You have to form a field large enough to pick real winners and real losers.

For example, if you look at the glass-container market, you might see that one particular company's sales were growing faster than those of a competitor. But unless you looked at the entire food-packaging market, you would have noticed that aseptic multilayered foil packaging was experiencing growth rates of several orders of magnitude higher than the rate of growth of the glass company, and that there was only one company making aseptic packaging. Which was the better investment: the glass company that was outpacing its competitors, or the aseptic-packaging company that was outpacing the entire industry? The latter seems the far better choice.

Often, though, the choices are not so clear-cut. You have to look at a lot of companies within an industry, and you have to broaden your definition of the industry so that you catch all the possible competitors. Sometimes, when you do that, your mind will want to divide the industry into subsectors.

Look at the packaging industry again. You could look at all types of packaging, or you could break it down into glass-container makers, steel-can manufacturers, aluminum-can makers, plastic container makers, cardboard-box manufacturers, and aseptic packagers. If you are truly obsessed with the packaging industry, breaking the industry down into subgroups is useful: It will provide you with three or four possible winners, each of which might rise a couple of percentage points vis-à-vis its competitors, and also give you one clear overall industry winner. But if you are like most of us, and you aren't in the packaging industry, the benefits of such exhaustive research are not likely to pay off as well.

This brings me to another point, which is not one of the Ten Immutable Laws of Marketplace Checks, but probably is a *component* of *each* of the laws: Research what you know. If you are a physician or a nurse, you're going to know a lot more about the drug, hospital, medical-device, and HMO industries than you are going to know about packaging or cars. You are going to have a wider range of contacts and be able to develop and check hypotheses from observations a lot more quickly in any medical field than you could check things out in other areas.

In addition, you are going to be attending conferences and meeting physicians and nurses and other health practitioners from other parts of the country, and they are going to be the people whom you want to get on your panels, since they can provide you with that wider range of feedback that you need to know whether you've spotted a trend or not.

Finally, when you stick to your own industry and a couple of related industries, you will know what the new products are going to be long before the general public, and you can begin to think about how their introduction may affect the existing marketing order.

Law #9: The Questions You Ask Determine the Answers You Get

This seems like common sense, but it is actually the hardest law to get right. It's one of the things we are constantly telling our reporters. Here's what we mean: Most people have a tendency to ask very specific, narrow questions because they don't know how to ask open-ended questions, and because they believe that they should not be wasting their source's time.

For example, let's say I work at a mid-sized company, and I'm having lunch with the head of the computer department. I ask him how he is handling wireless communication with his sales force. He tells me that not only is his system up and running, but that the management is now asking him to look ahead to see what he needs to do about implementing a companywide enterprise-resource-planning (ERP) system. I say, "Aha! ERP. I just saw a Microsoft commercial on TV where two managers on the go are talking at an airport, and one asks the other how his company implemented its ERP software. That must mean that ERP is going to be important."

This starts me down the ERP path. Who makes ERP software? What is it used for? How large is the market? Why does everyone want ERP, or do they? Which company is likeliest to be the big winner? What are the unintended consequences?

If I researched this like most people, I would find ten more people like the head of my computer department, and ask them if they are planning to buy or implement ERP software this year and, if so, whose software. I would have an answer, of sorts, but I wouldn't really know enough to make a good decision.

I really need to go back to the head of my company's computer department and say, "This ERP software you mentioned the other day. It sounds interesting. What is it used for?" And, as he began to tell me, he might throw in some other terms, such as supply-chain management, or customer-relationship management, and I would ask him some more questions about those, and how they all fit together.

At the end of our conversation, I would know that there are a couple of things that are likely to drive the sales of ERP software, and that there were markets for CRM (customer-relationship management) and SCM (supply-chain management) software as well, and that they all fit under the ERP umbrella. Then, if I did a little digging and found out that Siebel Systems and J. D. Edwards were market leaders, I would now have a basis for asking some more in-depth questions.

In-depth questions are open-ended questions. They are questions that begin, "Tell me about . . ." rather than "How many?" or "What kind?" They are questions that are designed to get a person talking, and to get that person to express an opinion, or to talk about his or her own hypothesis. If you ask, "Why do you think that is?" when people give you a fact, you will get their logic and reasoning as well as their answer. Often, you will come away a lot better informed.

Once you learn to ask open-ended questions, people wind up telling you a lot more than they thought they would—or should. You might call a computer-department head to talk about ERP software, and get some comments, and then find out when you ask him about implementation that his company cannot afford to make the investment right away. Some gentle questioning along the lines of "I guess there are other things you have to do first," or, "Gee, won't that leave you behind your competitor?" might yield an unexpected research dividend, such as that the company is having problems (like Hershey, with its inventory-management software). You might not be following that company, but now you have you a piece of information that you can trade with someone who is, or you can put some time into following the company more closely, to see if there is a selling opportunity.

When you ask tightly defined questions, you get only what you've asked about. When you learn to ask open-ended questions, you are starting conversations with people, and conversations can lead anywhere. One of the best open-ended questions is, "Is there anyone else you know of whom I should speak with?" Almost always, the person will give you the name and phone number of two or three colleagues within his industry, often at competitors. Before you call, ask your contact whether you can use his or her name. If so, that will open still more doors for you.

Law #10: Know When to Take Your Money off the Table

Remember the Kenny Rogers song, "The Gambler"? The last line of the chorus was, "You never count your money while you're sittin' at the table, there'll be time enough for countin', once the dealin's done." That's a handy rule to live by. When you come across a piece of information that no one else has, it's easy to imagine that you're about to make huge profits, and it's easy to become bitterly disappointed when you don't. It is difficult to ferret out truly valuable knowledge, and it is also difficult to take advantage of it. For example, you might go to a lot of trouble to develop a bit of knowledge, and then discover that the stock is overpriced even without your find. If the knowledge is upside news, the stock might not react at all, no matter how good the news is. At that point, you have to take your money off the table because that investment is not going to give you enough profit potential.

The same thing is true for downside news. I talked earlier about relativity (Law #8). If a company's sales are continuing to rise, but the momentum is decreasing, why do you want to wait until the next quarter, when everyone else discovers what you know, and analysts all over Wall Street begin to downgrade the stock.

When we disadvise large institutions, our discovery of a negative story is the advice our large institutional clients appreciate the most. When I was running Grassroots Research for Claude Rosenberg's RCM Capital Management, our ability to find companies whose momentum was slowing was considered a far greater benefit than the upside stories we could tell. That's because money managers can afford to look mediocre on the way up—as long as they are somewhere just ahead of the market averages, they will be rewarded—but they need to look brilliant when the market is on its way down. A money manager who can lock in a profit by getting out of a stock before it tanks is a real hero to his clients, who are all counting their paper profits in their heads.

Learn to develop the same kind of mentality. For every investment you make, begin to develop a time horizon for it. Reevaluate it constantly. If the company is in a volatile industry, you may have to make calls as often as every week, but usually, if you are calling your sources on a monthly basis, you will have ample forewarning of a problem that won't materialize until the current quarter is over and the company has released its numbers.

Do not wait for the bad news to overtake you. If you sell prematurely and the company's stock continues to rise, you can always find another investment. If you sell out too late, you are throwing money away.

13

What Comes, Goes

Notes on Selling Stock

Will Rogers once said that the way to make money in the stock market was to buy good stocks and watch them go up. If it was that easy, we'd all be millionaires without ever having to watch Regis Philbin. But stocks go down, too. They go down for all sorts of reasons and, as a marketplace checker, one of the ways you can beat the stock markets is to learn when and how to sell.

The most important reason to sell a stock is that it no longer meets the performance criteria that you've set for it. If, for example, you are looking for gains of at least 15 percent a year, any stock that fails to make that 15 percent hurdle rate should not be in your portfolio. You cannot waste your time and money by hoping that the stock will recover and rise. If you have been doing your marketplace checks properly, you will know whether the stock is going through a short correction phase, or whether it has simply outlived its usefulness to you.

The second thing you need to know about a stock is the relation of its price to its value. Everyone knows that there is something called a price/earnings ratio. But there is a price/value ratio as well.

Value is the amount of gain left in a stock. Let's take two companies, both of whose stocks are selling at $40 a share. Company A has had several quarters of increasing earnings, but its shares have not risen appreciably because the company is in an unpopular sector, like autos or chemicals. Company B is a pharmaceutical company whose shares have been rising steadily on only modest increases in earnings.

Which represents the better value? If the rate of earnings rise is greater than the price rise, so that the P/E is falling as the company gets stronger, there is increasing value in the company. It means that the market as a whole is not recognizing the value of the earnings increase or what it means both to the company and the industry as a whole. This is a buy opportunity. If the P/E is rising faster than earnings, there is declining value in the company. Calculate the value left in every stock you own, and set some targets for exiting them. That way, you won't be left with stocks that have made money for someone else, but have little chance of making money for you.

Probably the best example of this is Digital Equipment, a long-gone company. DEC once dominated the market for mid-sized computers. For years, DEC made almost all of its money by selling basic computers to resellers, who then added features that made them attractive to specific customer groups. In 1988, DEC decided that it, too, could sell to those customer groups, and it began to invest heavily in a sales force and in new products. Wall Street read DEC's efforts as positive, and began rewarding it with a higher and higher price/earnings multiple as sales rose. But unnoticed for more than three quarters was the fact that the cost of selling, plus the cost of all the new people, was rising at a far faster rate. In September 1988, the rise of expense finally overcame the rise in sales. The company reported a loss, the stock tanked, and it never recovered.

Selling stocks is an exercise in what Henry Kissinger used to call "realpolitik"—reality politics. There are a million reasons to buy any given stock, and just as many reasons for selling it. If you have been paying close attention to the information in this book, you already know many of them.

But let's reiterate:

A. Changes in management. Is General Electric going to be as good a company after Jack Welch retires? Welch has not only made GE a more profitable company, but has made some very subtle changes in the company's culture that has also made it a far better-run company. Before Welch took over, GE was one of the companies most fined by the federal government. It had suffered repeated bribery and price-fixing scandals, and had been fined for poor workplace practices of one sort or another by virtually every federal agency.

With more than 250,000 employees, GE's pre-Welch management felt that the reason for such behavior was simply that there are going to be some bad apples in such a large bunch. But Welch felt differently, and managed to make everyone in the company realize that cutting corners for any reason impacts the profitability of the company. Will that behavior continue under Jeffrey Immelt, Welsh's successor, or will he feel compelled to drive the employees harder, in order to prove that he is a better manager than Welch. The same thing is true for Michael Eisner at Disney, and for almost any chief executive who has had a long and profitable tenure. As Louis XV was reputed to have said, *Après moi le déluge.*

B. Changes in the economy. We are in the midst of the longest peacetime expansion in history, founded upon a seemingly insatiable thirst for productivity-improving high technology, in the form of computers, telecommunications equipment, and Internet hookups. From one vantage point, the good times are going to go on and on, almost indefinitely. Despite the installed base of computers, less than one person in ten in the

223

world is computer enabled, and about the same number are telephone enabled. That would seem to leave enormous room for growth in both markets.

But in the United States, which is the largest market by far, sales of computers, Internet connections and new telephone sales are reaching plateaus. If worldwide sales continue to grow, stock prices will continue to rise. If not, then who knows?

While those drivers of the economy are sending out mixed signals, other sectors are mixed as well. Energy prices have been rising after remaining low for a decade. New-car sales have roared along at a rate that is probably unsustainable. Prices of movie tickets are rising, but so are the costs of producing movies. After a brief fling with low-budget independent films, Hollywood is sinking its dollars into hugely expensive blockbusters again. If they pan out in the way *Mission: Impossible 2* has, that's fine. But most blockbusters will be more like the laughable *Battlefield Earth,* which went in and out of theaters faster than John Travolta could put on his makeup.

All of these, of course, pale alongside the decision by the Federal Reserve governors on what to do about interest rates. Each quarter-point rise takes tens of billions of dollars out of consumer spending, and puts those dollars into the hands of financial institutions, who raise their rates in sync with the Fed. The ripple effect of rising interest rates is so vast that it reaches into the tiniest crevices of the economy, marginalizing businesses and creating unemployment.

The impact of politics on the market cannot be underestimated. At least part of the price of stocks is based on future beliefs of a very large number of people, and if those beliefs change with the party in power, the stock markets rise or fall, irrespective of what is actually going on in the macroeconomy. But the macroeconomy changes as well, and not always as predicted. It is a general truism that Republicans favor low taxes, and that low taxes are good for the economy. But lately, as the baby boom has begun to age, paying down the national debt has begun to take on more significance than keeping taxes low. If consumer/voters perceive that a Republican administration is not going to pay much attention to the debt, their willingness to fuel the economy through spending may well diminish even more than it has due to rising interest rates.

C. Changes in company performance. As changes in the economy ripple outward, it produces an entirely new set of corporate winners and losers. As you raise interest rates, for example, businesses that depend upon "float"—being able to pay their bills out of cash flow instead of out of retained earnings— become more difficult to manage. Payments stretch out. Companies are more likely to book revenues as soon as a deal is signed, rather than as funds accrue, so that investors can expect to see an increasing number of accounting irregularities if the economy tightens.

Companies that have not been especially profitable even in good economic times will find that they are under even more pressure to merge for profitability. M&A activity will increase, rather than decrease. And with all of the changes that will come will come changes in investor expectations. When Internet stocks cratered on April 14, 2000, many analysts believed that it was just a temporary correction. But if investor expectations begin to shift into a lower gear, it is going to be more difficult to sustain the high performance levels of the late 1990s.

D. Changes in population characteristics. One of the great consequences of the stock-market boom of the past decade was that it enriched Americans, who are chronically poor savers. Through 401(k) plans, SEPs, and IRAs, as well as through stock option grants and the wealth creation of the Internet economy, more people have seen their savings balances rise than at any time in history. But as baby boomers continue to age, they are going to begin to become net consumers of income, rather than net savers. Right now, the stock market depends in part for its growth on the huge river of money that flows in daily from pension and other savings plans. But what happens when that money begins to flow out, first as interest, and then as accumulated capital? Few studies have been done which suggest the directions the economy might take in the future as the population ages. I'm an optimist about such things, but there really is no way of knowing.

E. A change in marketplace tastes. This is somewhat akin to changes in demographics, but it is both more and less than demographic shifting. Remember: Americans have an unquenchable thirst for the new. They are easily bored with the old. So a product that is selling well today may not sell so well tomorrow. Overall, a category may continue to improve, but the product leaders within it may be shifting continually. That forces you, as a marketplace checker, to be constantly on the lookout for these changes. Increasingly, more and more categories are coming to resemble the entertainment industry, with "top 10" lists that change every couple of weeks or months, driven along by relentless cycles of innovation, paired with intense consumer boredom.

F. Changes in channels. As competition within a category heats up, companies are always on the lookout for new places to sell their products, or more efficient ways to sell them. One of the reasons the Internet—and Internet stocks—took off was the expectation that there would be a major shift in buying patterns, and that companies could sell much more inexpensively over the Net.

Both expectations proved to be largely wrong. Net sales, while growing steadily, are a tiny fraction of overall consumer sales. Meanwhile, the cost of installing the infrastructure that make Net sales possible—everything from servers and routers and fiber-optic cables to huge automated warehouses—has made profitability elusive for all but a handful of Internet companies. Meanwhile, companies continue to pour funds into the development of alternate channels, offering incentives to consumers in the hopes that the channels will be used. When they are, it can signal a major competitive shift. When the new channels go unused, they signal an expensive investment that will kill profitability for at least a couple of quarters.

G. Changes in the world scene. During the 1980s, it was easy to talk about a First World, which consisted of a handful of nations (sometimes called the G-7 economies of the United States, Great Britain, France, West Germany, Japan, Canada, and Italy); a Second World consisting of smaller economies such as the Scandinavian countries, the Netherlands, Belgium, Austria, Australia, New Zealand, Israel, and the Soviet bloc states; and the rest of the nations, lumped together as an impoverished Third World.

That ranking system no longer holds. The United States stands alone as a First World state, based on incomes, national wealth, a stunningly low unemployment rate, an awesome job-creation rate and numerous other factors. The remainder of the G-7, perhaps with the exception of Canada and Italy, but with the inclusion of the Netherlands, have fallen to a second-tier status, still very comfortable, but no longer nearly as dynamic, and struggling with a host of problems. Belgium, Austria, Scandinavia, Canada, Italy, Australia, New Zealand, Israel and a handful of other nations, like Singapore and Taiwan, occupy a next rung: prosperous, but with economies too small to be major players.

And then the rungs get farther and farther apart, with space on the rung below for nations such as Argentina, Mexico,

Malaysia, Brazil, and Spain, and going down from there. Very large states like China and India have future potential, but their social and infrastructure problems are so large and require such huge spending that it is problematic whether the investments being made in those nations will ever yield the results that everyone hopes for.

And then there are the former Communist nations of eastern Europe—especially the former Soviet Union—which are going through their own growing pains.

No one knows where the next economic crisis will come from—or when.

All of these perspectives on change can have an impact not only directly on stock prices, but on the marketplaces where you are doing your checking. In an unsettled atmosphere, it will pay to be even more vigilant than you might have been in good economic times. The marketplace will bring more changes, not fewer, as every company struggles to achieve or retain a dominant position. That is why you have to look at every stock you own with a critical eye.

At OTR, the advice we give our institutional clients is far more valuable to them when they decide to sell than when they decide to buy. That is because, unlike you, institutional holders don't fall in love with the stocks they purchase for their portfolios. They are being judged every quarter on a comparative basis, their bonuses paid or not depending upon how well they do in relation to other firms and other money managers.

When *you* purchase a stock, you probably fall in love with it, and use all sorts of rationales to continue owning it when you should have dumped it months ago. Not so with institutions. They will own a stock only so long as it performs. We give them the clues that signal that a stock is about to begin performing in a manner that is below expectations. Knowing when to sell— not holding onto a stock for too long—can add as much as 15 percent to your annual performance.

But what about the stock that you sell which then goes on to become Wall Street's next darling? There are all sorts of anecdotes about that subject, and everyone knows someone who made a killing in the stock that you didn't hold on to long enough. My answer to you is, "So what?" If you are buying and selling stocks in order to have bragging rights on the golf course, you are always going to find someone who can one-up any story you tell. But presumably, you are investing in order to build your wealth, and one of the characteristics of wealth is modesty. You want to let people know about your marketplace-check discoveries *after* you have already made your investment because that will have a direct positive impact on the price of the shares you own. But you don't want to go around bragging about how much money you are making. It serves no point, and it takes you away from your objective, which is to improve your performance.

People tend to be optimistic about their purchases. That's not only true for stocks, but for most things. You buy a car because you think that it will satisfy your needs, and then you find out that you are unhappy. Very few people turn around and sell a car after a few weeks. In fact, people will hold onto even a defective car—a lemon—for years and years, looking for the good in their purchase even when it does not exist.

The same thing is true for stock buys, only more so. Most people put far too much of their ego into the stocks they buy. If they are getting a recommendation from a broker, they want to believe that the broker has their interests at heart. If they are picking their own stocks, they want to believe that their decisions were based on more than hunch, rumor, or the fact that their snotty brother-in-law claimed to be making money in the stock. As a consequence, investors do all sorts of weird things to justify their failing objectivity. Instead of attempting to find rationales and justifications for your purchases, learn to rely upon good information, the kind you are developing through a marketplace-check system.

That is the point of this entire book. When you began reading it, it was with the purpose of competing with the best minds on Wall Street, with the belief that if you could find a way to learn more, you could outsmart them and gain a superior return for yourself. If you've learned all the lessons of this book, learning how to sell will be the final, most important lesson, because the real money is made on not holding on to stocks past their prime.

14

CONCLUSION

In some respects, this book has rambled a bit. I've tried to put all of the information I think you need into it, and in the right order, but there are always bits and pieces that are left hanging. This last chapter pulls all of that loose string together into a neat little ball. Therefore, this chapter will show you how to put everything together, and to do it with confidence.

Way back at the beginning, I told you to set up a file-folder system, either on your computer or, if you feel more comfortable, in legal folders for each company that you were going to follow. Into those folders was going to go everything you could find out about the company, from information about its senior executives to financial data from the annual report, 10-K, and 10-Q, along with quarterly reports. (You would do best to have both types of folders, as some things (reports from the Internet) are more easily stored electronically by click, drag, and drop, and some things (like magazines articles, or brochures handed out at trade shows), can just be placed in an old-fashioned folder. It should also contain newspaper and magazine articles that pertain directly to your company or its competitors. In addition, all of your interviews and panel results should be in the folder. Within a year, your folders should be bulging.

231

Why all that information? To see patterns. Some very bright people can discern a pattern with only a couple of data points. But usually, the more data points you have, the clearer the picture becomes.

Think of the game show *Wheel of Fortune.* Every now and then, there is a phenomenal contestant who can guess the puzzle even before Vanna White has turned over the letters. On such a show, Pat Sajak might go through as many as eight puzzles in a half hour. On other shows, the contestants are really slow on the uptake, and Pat is lucky to make it through three puzzles. But generally, if you are a regular watcher, you'll notice that the average is about five puzzles per show. Some sayings will just pop right out at the contestants and the home audience, and others will take a bit longer. That's the way pattern recognition operates in the real world. You can train a cruise missile to recognize a target by matching it to photographs stored in its memory, but human beings have to sift through a lot more information than a cruise missile to recognize a target of opportunity. If you collect lots of information on a company, you'll have an easier time seeing larger patterns emerge.

Of course, you have to read the information that you collect. This is not an exercise in collecting the largest ball of aluminum foil; if the information you are collecting isn't being used to advance your knowledge of the companies you invest in, why are you bothering? I know this sounds too obvious to even require saying, but you'd be surprised at how many people become so taken up with the path that they forget their destination. Reading your files regularly enables you to not only see the patterns, but to see the holes in your knowledge.

While I don't believe that diversification in your portfolio does you much good, I do believe that diversification is essential in marketplace checking. OTR gets its information from primary sources; the buyers, customers, consumers, and retailers who are making the decisions about the products that translate into rising and falling sales. The portfolio managers we serve have their own sources of data, from information from the company, to trade publications, to other companies just like ours. We provide a service to them, but their job—what they get paid millions of dollars a year to do—is to pull the information together from disparate sources and turn it into buy and sell recommendations that will make their large institutional clients greater profits.

So Final Rule number one, is "Diversify your information sources." You want all the conventional sources you can find—company information, magazine and newspaper articles, even analysts' reports (more on those in a few minutes)—and you want the unconventional sources, the information that your team members and your panels provide. If your information is top-heavy with conventional sources, your chances of gleaning useful moneymaking information is almost nil. But if you don't have that information base, your chances of asking the right questions of the panels is *also* almost nil. Balance your information sources with enough secondary material so that you are knowledgeable on the surface, and a sufficient number of unconventional sources so you can plumb a subject in depth.

Final Rule number two has to be, "Organize your information." If you are pulling information on several companies from multiple sources, you are going to be overwhelmed quickly by the data you receive. You want to be able to use what you acquire, and make sense of it as quickly as possible, so it really helps to create a structure for your information. At Off The Record Research, we use a standardized reporting structure. You should develop some version of that structure, especially if you are sharing information with team members. Your reports need a title and topic sentence, just like the reports you wrote in high school and college. The title should include the company's name, and the topic sentence should tell you what the report is going to tell you.

You don't need to go into the journalistic "who, what, where, why and how" level of detail in the first paragraph, but your sentence ought to encapsulate the news you are about to impart. For example; "Competitors Clamor for Palm's Share." "Palm Inc. has enjoyed being the dominant personal digital assistant (PDA) player, but its inventory shortages have opened the door for Handspring Inc.'s Visor and Pocket PCs powered by Microsoft Corp.'s Windows." This headline and topic sentence tell you worlds about the PDA market, and make it easy for your team members to focus on the opportunity that could arise out of this situation.

Good headlines and topic sentences should write themselves. You'll know you're on the right track by how easily the headline and topic sentence of a report come to you. If the data are equivocal—the pattern has not emerged and is still a bit fuzzy—you are going to have a hard time convincing yourself or any member of your team that you have found a valuable nugget. I am not suggesting that you force the issue. That path leads to self-deception and error. If you don't have a positive or negative conclusion, you don't yet have a story, and without a story, you don't have an investment rationale.

This is not necessarily bad. If you are doing your checks properly, the lack of a conclusion should be a signal to do more digging, to make a few more phone calls, or to ask one of your experts for an interpretation. It might also be a signal that something is happening in the marketplace, but it is not altogether clear. When marketplaces are murky, when no clear winner emerges, then a new entrant is usually just around the corner.

This happens all the time. Two or three companies battle for market share, and then a fourth company comes along with an entirely new marketing proposition, or a new sales channel, or new technology, and takes over the marketplace. Dell Computers did it in the PC industry, pushing its way through a crowded field of leaders dominated by IBM, Apple, and Compaq. Nokia did it in cellular phones, which was a market dominated in the United States by Motorola. Mrs. Fields did it in chocolate-chip cookies, in a field dominated by Nabisco and Keebler, and Callaway did it in golf, in a field dominated by old-line sporting-goods manufacturers like Spalding and Rawlings.

Organizing your information also forces you to come to some conclusions about your information and to match it to real-world conditions. Earlier, I mentioned that you might want to start your marketplace-check system by making some imaginary buy and sell decisions, so you could get some feel for the company you are tracking. Part of that feel involves learning to see what Wall Street knows and doesn't know. If you make an imaginary investment and the stock moves up after you have made your investment, you obviously are ahead of the analysts. The time interval between when you buy and when the stock moves upward is your cushion.

If the stock doesn't move up, watch it for a while. Few things remain undiscovered for long. If the stock moves downward when you think it should have moved upward, go back and question both your data and your sources. If your sources reconfirm what they told you, and additional sources continue to give you the same information, it pays to wait.

Final Rule number three is "Teamwork counts." I have talked about you as a lone individual for much of this book, even though I spoke about teams in the beginning. When I talk to each reader individually, I expect that you will find some way to form teams or groups.

The best kind of group is an investment club. There are tens of thousands of these clubs around the country, and they are easy to form. Overwhelmingly, today's clubs are neighborhood affairs, but in today's Internet world, and with cheap long-distance telephone rates, there is no reason that locality should be a barrier to forming teams in the future. With Internet banking and friendly brokers who are more than willing to handle the paperwork and trades for a club, there is nothing to stop you from organizing a club that exists solely in cyberspace. As long as only one of your team has the ultimate buy-and-sell authority, you should have as little problem functioning across the country as you would if you were having a weekly meeting with your neighbors in your kitchen.

We spend a lot of time taking care of our reporters. Our editors take the time to discuss investment ideas with them, and we are hunting constantly for information that we can send out to a reporter to make his or her job easier. As a team leader, you ought to be doing the same thing. You should be sharing the contents of your legal file with all of the members of your team, and they should be sharing the contents of their folders with you. There is an old saying that many heads are better than one (except, as one wag put it, if they are all on the same person), and the more you can get your team members to cooperate, the greater the likelihood that you will produce results that will pay off in good investment ideas.

Just as we take care of our reporters, you should take care of your team members and your sources. Aside from the thank-you notes and small gifts that we send, we also get our reporters together once a year at a fun location (we've done this in New Orleans, New York, and Palm Springs, among other places) so we can compare methodology notes, improve our learning and have a little fun. If you are running a far-flung group, or even if you are running a group made up of neighbors, you might want to plan a little "retreat" once a year. This exercise will allow you some time to get into your subject in a much deeper manner, and to iron out any of the kinks in your reporting system.

Now the downside. Not every reporter who works for us works out. Marketplace checking is a demanding existence, and sometimes even the best reporters find themselves stymied or simply unable to make the right connections in their area. When that happens repeatedly, we find that not only are we unhappy, but so are the reporters. They then go on to other work, and are usually more content. Not only is it best for them, it's best for us because our business depends upon our having the best information for our clients. You have to take much the same path. It is not unusual for investment-club members to come and go when they disagree with the investment objectives of the club.

If you decide to organize along marketplace-checking lines, do not hesitate to hold every member accountable in some way. People have to meet deadlines, especially if you want to trade on a regular basis. People have to find a way to get the information they need, even if it means running up their phone bills a bit. And your team members have to organize the data accurately and ask the same questions that everybody else is asking. As the team leader, you must take the responsibility of getting materials—especially questionnaires—to team members, on a timely basis, so they have as much leeway as possible in getting their reports done. If you are going to make this work, you have to work. As Woody Allen once said about the entertainment industry, "It's called show *business,* not show show."

The Final Final Rule is, "Have fun." I do marketplace checks because I found it one of the most intellectually challenging—and enjoyable—ways that I could make money. I might have become a money manager, but there are thousands of money managers, all being judged harshly by the standards of the marketplace. Their results are "marked to market" at the end of every business day, and managers who do not perform do not last long.

I will not kid you into thinking that marketplace checks are a lazy person's way to riches. Everything I've told you ought to convince you otherwise. But if you agree with my premise that you are surrounded by information, then picking out the right nuggets is a lot like being in an orchard and finding the best tree with the best fruit. The fruit is out there, and you will find it if you look for it.

You have an advantage that the vast majority of investors will never have. By doing the marketplace checks described in this book, you will gain some independent corroboration of what the stock markets are telling you. That alone will make you a better investor, even if you never turn up a nugget of information. You will become more skeptical of what you hear, more astute in interpreting events, and more knowledgeable about how the world works. That's a good investment in and of itself. If you make money as well, you will really be ahead of the game.

ACKNOWLEDGMENTS

When you decide to write a book that challenges the way people invest their money in stocks and suggest a better way, you have many people to thank. First, I would like to thank Marty Baron, my dear friend and executive editor of **The Miami Herald,** for suggesting the idea of doing a book on marketplace checks for retail investors. John Mahaney, my editor at Crown Business, has been wonderfully patient as both Steve and I went through the drafts and redrafts. Thanks again to my agent, Marc Reiter, who knew a good idea when he saw it.

Writing and researching the book would have never happened without my close friend and associate Jeffery Yudkoff. Jeffery, I owe you one, and on your book I hope I can do as much work as you have done on mine. To all the wonderful people who have worked at OTA Off The Record Research and made it successful, this book is an embodiment of your spirit to change the world of investing: I wish I could mention you all, but I do want to thank my brother, Geoff Gordon, Annie Fountain, Jon Gates, Allison Malone, Margaret Bennett, Katie Sanborn, Donna Crothers, Sandee McCready, Hartmut Leuschner, and Liz Frey. You know how much you have done to move this idea forward. Our mission to make sure investors are using marketplace checks just expanded to a bigger audience.

To Joann Steck-Bayat, Darryl Forman, and the late Mimi Kassarjian (whom I think of every day): You helped start the process, and we really never had a chance to make this as big as it could have been inside RCM Capital Management.

To the believers at my first investment job—Joe Mark, Rust Muirhead, John Kriewal, and Gary Schreyer—challenging existing notions in a powerful company was a great risk, and you helped me feel more confident.

And I certainly will never forget Claude Rosenberg, the true originator of the Grassroots concept. Claude, your innovativeness and original thinking will always be a part of my life; I hope I can continue your proud tradition of constantly refining the research process for buying and selling stocks.

I must mention all of the customers of OTA Off The Record Research who were willing to risk trying something new. Funny how obvious that sounds now, but it wasn't so long ago that the traditional Wall Street approach to research and the buddy system in trading stonewalled different approaches. There are many names here, and I apologize in advance for having forgotten some, but I especially want to thank Stan Druckenmiller, who showed me how to take unique information and make the big bet (Stan, no one I have ever seen is better at this than you are); Joe DiMenna and Brenda Earl, who besides being great friends are the best at recognizing when a piece of information that comes across their desks is unique and actionable; Scott Bessent, who had the insight to use this information around the world looking for advantages; Joe Barsky, who always inspired good ideas to research during talks in his office; and all of the people at Friess Associates—especially Foster Friess, Andy Graves, and Bill D'Alonzo—where field checks of customers are a way of life.

A special note of appreciation goes to my first customers, Ron Ognar at Strong Capital Management and Beth Terrana at Fidelity Investments. Ron, you always have been someone who digs deeper for the true story about a stock than others did.

Thanks for making sure our information helped keep you ahead of your peers. Beth, you truly are one of the greatest portfolio managers I have ever worked with. Your ability to cut through information overload and realize what is important and to honestly question yourself when things change are two characteristics I hope you can instill in the Fidelity managers you work with. To me, when you exercised these talents, you were unmatched in your ability to manage money.

A number of business associates have also helped during the years I have been doing this: Clark Johnson, you took a chance with me on Pier 1 Imports' board when others hadn't even heard the idea of marketplace checks; Barry Wish, every time I see you I come back thinking I need to talk more to you and am filled with enthusiasm to conquer the world; Harris Barton, who looked at me across a breakfast table and said, "Craig, you have to start your own business. It is the next step"; Jane Barber, one of the original investors; Dick Elden, who believes as I do that investigative skills are much needed on Wall Street; and, finally, Marty Berman, my mentor and true friend. Marty, someday I want to write a book about all you have taught me about business. You are a true mensch.

Kevin Heneghan and Ira Leventhal, without you two I probably would be back teaching. The way you run a business is an inspiration to all. Kevin, you are one in a million because you truly let the people you work with grow while keeping them on the tried and true path. I would go to war with you anytime.

Finally, a note to my wife, Nanette, and my wonderful family, which includes her mother and father, Mary and Paul Vogelheim; my sons, Richie and Eric; my brother Geoff (already mentioned above); my best buddy Keith; and my sister Diane. Nano, you are the one who said the challenge of writing a book would be good for me; sometimes I think you know me better than I do. One of my big regrets in life is that my father and mother did not get to know you when they were in the prime of their lives. You have the wonderful ability of making anyone who is close to you a better person.

To all, thanks again, we are just at the beginning of changing the way people buy and sell stocks . . . the next few years are sure going to be exciting!

INDEX

ABOUT THE AUTHORS

Craig Gordon is the general partner of OTA Limited Partnership and Director of its Research division OTA/Off The Record Research that has revolutionized the way equity research is done. Mr. Gordon directs a team of 180 seasoned industry analysts who provide unbiased marketplace checks on specific stocks. By verifying—or disputing—Wall Street assumptions about specific industry trends and expectations about individual company performance, OTA/Off The Record Research provides a unique "bottoms-up" approach to information gathering and analysis that provides institutional money managers with a decided competitive edge in picking winning stocks.

Previously, Mr. Gordon was director of Grassroots research for RCM Capital Management and taught marketing at the University of California at Berkeley and Golden Gate University. He also has been a newspaper reporter. Mr. Gordon was a Rhodes scholar nominee and received his B.S. from Lehigh University and his M.B.A. from Yale University.

Mr. Gordon has served on several boards of companies and is active in the San Francisco Comicle, a charitable enterprise that raises money for community programs. He resides with his family in San Francisco.

Stephen Kindel is a former senior editor of *Forbes* and *Financial World*.

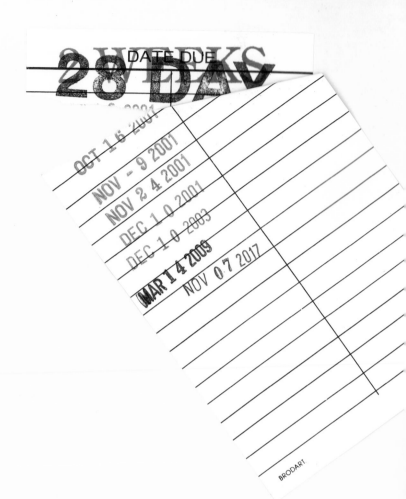